101 NUGGETS

OF TRUTH ABOUT YOUR MARRIAGE

Harry Nze

101 NUGGETS OF TRUTH ABOUT YOUR MARRIAGE

iUniverse books may be ordered through booksellers or by contacting:

iUniverse
1663 Liberty Drive
Bloomington, IN 47403
www.iuniverse.com
844-349-9409

Scripture quotations marked KJV are from the Holy Bible, King James Version (Authorized Version). First published in 1611. Quoted from the KJV Classic Reference Bible, Copyright © 1983 by The Zondervan Corporation.

ISBN: 978-1-6632-3765-1 (sc)
ISBN: 978-1-6632-3766-8 (e)

Library of Congress Control Number: 2022905287

Print information available on the last page.

iUniverse rev. date: 07/13/2023

Dedication

The bible talks about friends who are closer than a brother.
The bible was actually talking about my following friends:
Pastor and Mrs Mosley and Christy Ogbanga
Brother and Sister Telema & Enesima Briggs
Brother and SIster Remi Craig

SPECIAL FRIENDS:
Brother Vincent and Sister Jocelyne Egharavba
Victory Community Church Family

MY VERY SPECIAL HOUSEHOLD:
Angela O. Nze
Tobechi C. Nze
Chikerendu Nze-Oko
Amarachi-Nze Igwe Kalu
Ojinichika Nze
Shallom Nachi-Nze

IN MEMORIAM:
Ambassador Okebaram Ndubisi Nze

FRONT COVER PIX:
Thanks to Chaze and Ch-Chi Nze and kids

Endorsement

Pastor Harry Tobechi Nze is first and foremost a practicing Christian with unequivocal Integrity. Within Seven years of his Charismatic leadership of the Living Word Christian Men's forum, he revolutionized family life of men and women. He took couples from passive relationship to vibrant and joyful family living. He restored love and trust in many families through teachings under happy atmosphere that returned God's glory to homes.

Pastor Harry has a unique way of handling and applying the word of God in such a way that never leaves the memory of his listeners. In **101 NUGGETS OF TRUTH ABOUT YOUR MARRIAGE,** he shares soul-searching and eternal truth that can revolutionize any ailing marriage. The onus is with each couple to read this book line after line and precept after precept, imbibe its living content and make their marriage work!

One of his greatest points in this book is that you don't fall and remain on the floor. Life is all about maintenance and repair. You can get up and put back life into your marriage through meekness, humility and the instrumentality of forgiveness and reconciliation.

This book is worth reading because the author writes out of an overflow of true life knowledge of men and women he led first hand over the years.

Bro Emma Okorie,
President, Living Word Ministries,
Chancellor, Rhema University

The book, 101 NUGGETS OF TRUTH ABOUT YOUR MARRIAGE is a creative and yet biblically sound work of an imaginative writer. It draws out tremendous lessons for all involved in marriage relationship and those intending to get in. Much more, this book shows with no ambiguity that marriage not only originated from God; but to be entered into according to His prescription-between man and woman; husband to love his wife as Christ loves the church and wife to submit to the husband, being a helpmate to him.

This book will profit all, for there are lessons for all: married or unmarried, enjoying or enduring the marriage relationship, parents and children all have a place in this spirit-led book. I wholeheartedly recommend this great work to all.

DR. JUDE EHIEMERE

This book, 101 NUGGETS OF TRUTH ABOUT YOUR MARRIAGE is a deep rhema revelation given to Pastor Harry Nze by the Spirit of God. Pastor Harry opened my eyes to vital nuggets of invaluable knowledge. His writing style, knowledge and perspective is rare and very unique. This has caused me to make what I may call a 'paradigm shift' from my traditional beliefs and opinion about marriage I have been brought to a point where I wish readers should have a vision for their marriages and pursue it with the tenacity. Such tenacity will overthrow failure, buttressing it as an opportunity to positively start again.

Readers will learn through this book that marriage is a hands-on-partnership in which all partners are expected to enter into with the aim of fulfilling God's eternal plan. I recommend this book to those who not only need "knowledge" but "therapy" for blissful everlasting marriage.

Martins Erondu,
Senior Pastor, Cross power Pentecostal ministries International
South Africa.

I have gone through the book and I must commend you for such a piece put together to take our marriages to another level. Every topic treated in the book is an essential recipe that will move ailing and hurting marriages forward and avoid marital limbo. I am so happy you touched every aspect of thorny issues we see in our modern marriages. This book addresses such issues to educate couples, irrespective of religious affiliations.

Tony Williams

101 NUGGETS OF TRUTH ABOUT YOUR MARRIAGE is an eye opener! I am honored to have read it. Every of the 101 nuggets is loaded with wisdom which can only come from God. In my candid opinion, the book should be made available to every couple on earth.

I have learnt powerful secrets of being a loving husband and godly father.

Ikwuagwu Igwe Kalu
Architect and pastor
Young Aflame Fellowship
Living Word Ministries, Abuja

The book, 101 NUGGETS OF TRUTH ABOUT YOUR MARRIAGE is a masterpiece. Every line, paragraph and page will arouse the reader's curiosity in an increasing crescendo. This book contains answers to questions of hot waters in marriage. You will certainly become a better husband or wife after reading this book.

John Bello
Editor and Publisher,
Freedom Press,
Oyo State, Nigeria.

Contents

Take Back Child Prarenting from the Government

The government took over parenting of the child and handed it over to the Television, Technology, Social media and Internet, thus disenfranchising parents' right to 'command' their children according to Genesis 18:19. Consequently, parents relinquished their rights to teach and train the child. Let us refer to the scripture to find out God's idea of parenting:

> *'For I know him, that he will command his children and his household after him, and they shall keep the way of the LORD, to do justice and judgment; that the LORD may bring upon Abraham that which he hath spoken of him'* – Gen. 18:19

God was proud of Abraham because he could 'command' his children instead of allowing the State to do so. No wonder He called Abraham friend. Are you a friend of God? It is not by merely singing and dancing about it. We can sing, clap and dance in church and call ourselves friends of God but have you asked yourself why God called Abraham His friend? Again, understand that it was not Abraham who called himself friend of God as we often say and sing. It was God who called him 'friend'. Can God call you 'friend?'

> *'Art not thou our God, who didst drive out the inhabitants of this land before thy people Israel, and gavest it to the seed of Abraham thy friend forever?'* – 2 Chron. 20:7

Can God vouch for you like He vouched for Abraham and Job? Abraham had a very close relationship with God. He was faithful in His walk with God. God boasted about Abraham: 'I KNOW HIM' that he will COMMAND his children and household…and they shall keep the way of the Lord. Can God boast of you? What legacy are you giving your children? Good food, good wardrobe and good education? These are not enough to attract the attention of God. You must snatch your children back from the government and teach them to keep the way of the Lord. You must make them have control over the television, technology, social media and internet. Right now, children are under the control of these. They must not be slaves but masters! Teach them to keep the way of the Lord and you have succeeded in making them be in control of the television, technology, social media and internet! This is one of the ways you can radicalize your marriage and make it positive.

Listen to me, the internet is a WWW: World Wide Web but today, it has become a wide wild world. You can make your children see it as a world wide web. If you can make them be in control, they will see it this way. But if you fail to COMMAND them and make them be in control, they will see it as a wide wild world and become lost in the perversion and corruption associated with internet. The ball is in your court. You have the prerogative of power save your children.

Be the Search Engine in the Family

Children are very inquisitive. They have too many questions to ask and too many problems to solve. These days, they no longer ask their parents questions. They would rather turn to the internet to find answers to their questions and solution to their problems. And to make a bad matter worse, they now attempt to teach their parents.

As parents, you can arrest this lazy approach to answers by building your knowledge capacity and proffer answers to their questions. Encourage them to interact with you and be free to ask you questions no matter how stupid! Distract them making the internet their first option when they seeking information. This way, you will achieve two things: first, you will have their attention more than the internet does. Second, you will have more influence over them. The influence of the internet is both positive and negative.

Be their search engine! Let your children trust you more than internet. At home, be the teacher they cherish like the teacher in the school. It may interest you to know that children believe and trust their teachers even more than their parents. You've got to win their faith and trust like their teachers at school. Start early by drawing them close. Teach them early what they should know before their peers lead them astray. Sex education is one of such lessons they must take from you. Teach them moral values.

Teach them that there are two types of body parts: private and public. Teach them that privates parts are parts no one should touch, look at or play with and such parts include: penis, scrotum, anus, laps, and buttocks (Male) and vaginal, breasts, anus, laps and buttocks (Female). Teach them is constitutes abuse for people to touch, see or play with these private parts. As the children grow, teach them more about sexuality. Make them ask you any question about sex. Be smart, move ahead of them and educate them properly before they stumble at facts (right or wrong) in the internet.

Train Your Children According to the Word of God

3

'Train up a child in the way he should go: and when he is old, he will not depart from it' – Prov. 22:6

God is the initiator of marriage and family. Thus, He has the blue print of how this great institution should be run. He tells us in proverbs 22:6 to **TRAIN** the children. Families are under intense attacks by the hordes of hell. Satan knows that desecrating this holy institution will bring dishonor to God. But as long as we refer to the bible, God will fix whatever challenges we face. As a member of the body of Christ and a model of his character, we must uphold the values designed for the family institution.

Values are ideals, customs and norms of a society towards which the people of the group have effective regards. These ideals can be positive or negative. The orientations and ideals you have accepted as norm and the values upon which you build must be in line with the word of God or else we would have a different view from the mind of God.

In Luke 4, Jesus went into the temple as his norm, custom or ideal was. There was a sense of value in him that drove him into the synagogue. This brings us back to the family. Where did Jesus get this value from? How did he know he had to be in the temple? It is certain that there was parental guidance. There was a godly family orientation. He must have been thoroughly taught to love and honour God the Father.

There is world of difference between **TEACHING** and **TRAINING**. The academic **teaching** children get from school is different from the moral values they need to be compatriots. This is what **training** does. The first and ideal place to inculcate this training is the home. Parents, especially fathers have largely failed to follow the Biblical injunction in proverbs 22:6 to train the child in the right ways. The government has succeeded in **TEACHING** the child including their rights to disobey and call the police when the parents attempt to train and punish them in order for them to learn and develop perfectly!

Do you want to radicalize your marriage and make your home a citadel of ethical and moral uprightness? Take over your children and **TRAIN** them in the way they should go so that they will not depart from it and become outlaws when they are full grown adults.

Pass on the Training You Received

4

It is very obvious that some centuries before now, parents inculcated excellent value system. Going down the memory lane when the technology we have today was absent, great grandfathers bequeathed these excellent values to their children who in this case are grandfathers. The values they imbibed were transferred to their children who in this case are fathers. This is where we are today. What values are we inculcating to our children today? Are they the values we imbibed or those the devil planted by taking advantage of technology? Today, LGBT is thriving because of the degraded moral values children of this century have. In the good old days, children were taught to pray even in the school! Almost all the sound values of those days have been reversed nowadays. There is need for urgent measures to save the family and by extension the church and state. It begins with you!

> *'And the things that thou hast heard of me among many witnesses, the same commit thou to faithful men, who shall be able to teach others also'* – 2 Tim. 2:2

Look at the Biblical method of transferring knowledge. Apostle Paul told Timothy to transfer the lessons he has imbibed from him to faithful men who should also transfer it to others. In other words, transference of values from great grandfather to grandfather, father and children. This should be our approach if we can ever reverse this ugly moral decadence in our depraved society today. Fathers and mothers should train their children with the training they received from their parents. This is the legacy they can bequeath to snatch their children from the government and societal depravity. And this is what we can do to radicalize our marriage and home to make it positive and impactful.

Sex and Food are Different from Respect

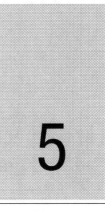

5

There are three things a man cherishes in life. They are sex, food and respect. On sex, it is true that man needs **many women** for only **one thing**: SEX. A woman needs **only one man** for **many things**. Man is moved by sight; the sight of a woman. He is easily seduced by the shape he sees in the front and back. He is moved by her eye lashes, hairdo and her physical infrastructure.

Also man cherishes food a lot. Of course he needs to eat well to perform his conjugal duty. He cares about his physical well-being as the bread winner. He hates to break down so that he doesn't fall short in his onerous responsibility as the head of the family.

And indeed, man needs respect. Ever heard of this thing called ego? Man has it in abundance. He seeks self-respect and the respect of others, especially women. Whether at home or in the office, man seeks to be respected.

The mistake many women do is that they place the cart before the horse. ***Women would rather serve their husbands food and sex before respect***. The Bible says Faith, hope and love but the greatest of the three is love. Now, food, sex and respect: the greatest of the trio is respect.

Let Respect Precede Sex and Food

6

'Wives, submit yourselves unto your own husbands, as unto the Lord. For the husband is the head of the wife, even as Christ is the head of the church: and he is the saviour of the body. Therefore as the church is subject unto Christ, so let the wives be to their own husbands in everything'- Eph. 5:22-24

In order to radicalize your marriage and make it positive, let women serve their husbands respect first before food and sex. With respect in his kitty, the man will provide more money for food and he will go the extra mile to satisfy her on the bed! Respect should therefore precede food and sex. It is respect that will bring the best out of a man.

It is a commonplace attitude in Africa that when a woman respects her husband, particularly when she praises him, he can go the extra mile to meet her needs. He will be disposed to shower money on her. It will be like asking her to name her price. Let every woman keep this secret and get more financial and material benefits from her husband. The home will certainly be healthier and better.

Love Your In-Laws

Food has ceased to be the fastest route to a man's heart because he can use the drive-through of any restaurant. The fastest route to your husband's heart is through loving his parents. Isaac brought Rebecca into his mother's kitchen.

'And Isaac brought her into his mother Sarah's tent, and took Rebekah, and she became his wife; and he loved her: and Isaac was comforted after his mother's death' – Gen. 24:67

A man's love for his wife will be beyond the realms of human understanding if she knows the secret of currying that love. Love his mother and he will love you back, good measure, pressed down, shaken together and running over. His love for you will supersede the love you have for his mother. He knows when you pretend to love his mother. And he knows if your love is genuine. Remember he was first with his mother before being with you now. Remember he suck his mother's breast before he fondles with yours. His mother has a special place in his heart. If you love her, he will love you abundantly. And your home will be a haven of peace and joy.

Sustain His Spirituality

8

Never let him drop from the level of spirituality you found him. Rather, humbly draw him up. Don't run him down and don't ruin him but raise him up. Be his spiritual boost. Be interested in spiritual things and don't be merely materialistic. Pray together. Share the word of God with him. Guard him jealously from whatever and whoever seeks to draw him away from God.

God gave man authority to dominate and lead but left the power of influence with the woman. Some women use this power effectively. Wives, do not abuse the power like Eve did. Use the power to make your husband to obey God rather than disobey. Use the power of influence to make your man wait upon the Lord, pray, study the Bible, make godly decisions and generally love God. Your home will be positive and full of love.

Stay Beside and Not Behind Him 9

The days of *'Behind a successful man is a woman'* are over. Today, *'Beside a successful man is a woman'*. Every woman has to be beside her husband in order to reach his ears on either side. His ears are not at his behind but besides him. Radicalizing your marriage to make it positive is what every woman can do when she takes her place beside him.

> *'And the LORD God caused a deep sleep to fall upon Adam and he slept: and he took one of his ribs, and closed up the flesh instead thereof; And the rib, which the LORD God had taken from man, made he a woman, and brought her unto the man. And Adam said, This is now bone of my bones, and flesh of my flesh: she shall be called Woman, because she was taken out of Man. Therefore shall a man leave his father and his mother, and shall cleave unto his wife: and they shall be one flesh'*- Gen.2:21-24

In the beginning, God created Adam. He was in the company of animals without the woman. One day, God showed up and made him come under His spiritual anesthesia. In that deep sleep, God brought out a rib from him with which He made into a woman. Notice carefully, according to scriptures that God did not bring out the rib from his head. God did not also bring out the rib from his foot. God brought out the rib from his side. When God made the woman, she was meant to be a help meet for him; suitable, fit, proper and equal with him.

The word 'helper' according to the Bible means "matching him and supplying what he lacks". The woman was not made out of his head to top him, not out of his feet to be trampled upon by him, but out of his side to be equal with him, under his arm to be protected, and near his heart to be loved.

Wives must be submissive to their husbands according to the word of God but husbands are urged to exercise their authority with caution not to manipulate woman but to love them and support them. Remember she was carved out of man's side. The Biblical teaching of submission is not slavery advocacy. Man and woman are meant to complement each other, though, they have different roles. The bottom line for every couple is STAY SIDE BY SIDE. This is a sure way to have a great marriage.

Stay Away from Bad Company

10

'Be not thou envious against evil men, neither desire to be with them'- Prov. 24:1, KJV

'Don't envy bad people; don't even want to be around them' – Prov. 24:1, MSG.

Your marriage will either be sustained or destroyed by the company you keep. It is your prerogative to choose your company. The instruction here is beware of bad company. Don't be envious of evil people. The Message translation says not to even be around them. It is akin to the instruction in the Bible that urges us to flee every appearance of evil. Look at what the Bible says elsewhere:

'Blessed is the man that walketh not in the counsel of the ungodly, nor standeth in the way of sinners, nor sitteth in the seat of the scornful' – Psalms 1:1

There are bad people; people who don't value relationships. They are exploiters and cheaters and they just take advantage of the other person. Now don't keep company with such people, don't keep company with evil men who are sexual perverts; people who must have cluster of women to satisfy their sexual urge; people who don't see anything wrong in extra-marital affairs or divorce.

Don't keep company with people that do not fear your God, don't keep company with people who have courage to do evil and are not pricked by their consciences. Apart from not keeping company with them, don't dare envy them. They are a bad model. The issue of envy is very critical here. There are people who are corrupt, immoral and ungodly who prosper. For the moment, they live large. Everything seems to go on well with them. Beware of such people. Don't envy them because they will not go too far. Evil will succumb in the long run.

The damage bad company has caused people is immeasurable. The Bible rightly warns that evil communication corrupts good manners. Because of bad company, several marriages have crashed abruptly. There are marriages that lasted only four months because of the influence of bad company. There are marriages that lasted only one month for the same reason. There are even marriages that did not last beyond 72 hours! A marriage crashed in 24 hours. They separated as soon as they were joined. From their honeymoon, each person moved away and never returned. Don't keep company with such people. They will corrupt your marriage if you are carefree.

Give More Attention to Your Household

11

In this 21st century, the issue of marriage is often treated with acute cynicism and humanistic opinions but this does not change the fact that marriage is God's idea and its purpose is certainly better defined by the Creator. The rate of divorce all over the world is alarming. This is largely due to the cynicism and humanistic opinion about marriage. According to polls by the Barna Research Group done several years ago, divorce rate in America is about 51%. It certainly hasn't improved today.

The marriage institution is ordained by God. It began with Adam and Eve in the Garden of Eden. God conceived it, made Eve from the rib of Adam and brought her to him. From that day, they were companions; husband and wife. Their relationship thrived and God blessed them with the fruit of the womb.

> *'For this cause shall a man leave his father and mother, and shall be joined unto his wife, and they two shall be one flesh. This is a great mystery: but I speak concerning Christ and the church'* – Eph. 5:31-32

God instituted and ordained marriage for a purpose which we must endeavour to preserve. In order to lead successful marriages, you must focus more on your household; your family of procreation than extended family; your family of orientation. Some foolish men pay more attention to the extended family at the detriment of the nuclear family which is your household. God is more interested in your household than the larger family. So spend more to nurture your household. Give more attention and invest more of your resources and time. This is how to radicalize your marriage.

Breast Feeding is Important

12

There are several benefits of breastfeeding. It supplies all the necessary nutrients in the proper proportions. It protects against allergies and sickness. It is easily digestible. Babies have healthier weights as they grow. Breastfed babies have higher scores in IQ tests. There are other benefits of this mother to child milk.

There is a special benefit of breastfeeding which is very essential in the overall well-being of the home. This is called **EYE TO EYE BONDING**. The eye to eye bonding between mother and child during breastfeeding is everlasting. The eye to eye bonding makes it easy for children to obey their parents in the Lord. It makes children to have high moral values and excellent value system. Children well breastfed hardly become out-law.

Making the marriage great does not exclude the children. When children are well brought up, they add to the bliss and the ambience of the home. When next you want to jettison breastfeeding, remember that eye to eye bonding during breastfeeding is very significant. It may just be the tonic to sustain a happy home.

Woman, Understand His Upbringing

13

Like I said before, there is a special bonding between mother and child during breastfeeding. So, there is a special bond between your husband and his mother. Understand therefore that every husband had been married before literally to his mother before getting married to his wife. This is not so between a father and daughter. That daily eye to eye bonding during breastfeeding is very significant. Now, getting married to his wife is a second experience. He expects that eye to eye bonding he had when he was a baby. He wants a repeat of that care and love.

To get the best out of him, every woman will do well to know how he grew up under his mother. If you can get this secret unraveled, you have won your husband completely. He will be a darling to you as he was to his mother. This one of the nuggets of truth you need to make your marriage great again.

Treat Your Wife as Your Daughter

14

Your wife is literally your first daughter before your first daughter. She therefore deserves to be treated as such. It is generally believed that fathers are fond of their daughters and the boys are closer to their mother. As a man, you know how much you love and care for your daughters. You have a soft spot for them. You are always there to protect them from intimidation. You always make enough provision for them so that they don't look elsewhere, especially to boys and men out there. Your daughters are special to you, isn't it?

Now, your wife is your first daughter before your first daughter. She too deserves to be loved and cared for. She deserves that tender loving care. She holds a special spot in your heart. She deserves to be protected, projected and preserved. She deserves your special attention. Treat her like your first daughter.

Moreover, remember the Garden of Eden? Eve was brought out of the side of Adam. So, every man should be a father to his wife. Eve came out of the side of Adam. His rib is close to his heart. As a man keep your wife close to your heart. She deserves to be loved and cuddled. She deserves your tender loving care. Your marriage will be great if you treat her as your first daughter.

Leave And Cleave

15

Some men are tied to their mother's apron long after they tie the nuptial cord. No, you can't be tied to two women. You must leave one for the other. This is what the Bible prescribes. You will tear yourself apart if you remain tied to your mother while you make a tie with your wife.

> 'Therefore shall a man leave his father and his mother, and shall cleave unto his wife: and they shall be one flesh'- Gen. 2:24

Two prominent words are used: leave and cleave. You cannot properly cleave until you leave. So, leaving precedes cleaving. Leave your father and mother first before cleaving to your wife. The Bible is not talking of severing your relationship with your parents. What the word of God means here is that you have a new home now. Your secrets belong to your new home. Your attention is more needed in your new home now. Your time, money, energy and all are needed in your new home now. You still love and care for your parents but your new cleavage is to your wife. You cleaved to your mother before, you must cleave to your wife now. Leave her in order to cleave to her. Shalom!

She Left All to Follow You

Your wife has brought so much to the table. You left your father and mother with something: their name. She left her father and mother with nothing, absolutely nothing! Her father spent so much to nurture and prepare her for you. Now, she has left her haven of love and joined you. She left behind her siblings, her father and mother. She left behind her father's name. No longer would she be called by her father's name.

Her identity is lost in you! She is now Mrs. Your name. This is a lot of sacrifice! Whereas, she was pampered in her family, you want her to pamper you now. Please pamper her as much. She deserves it. Pamper her like her father use to do. Protect her, project her and preserve her. Let her not be lost in you, she has already be lost in her father. Let her rather be found in you. Give her a better name. Let her be proud of you. Let her find a new father in you. Amen!

Treat Him Like Your Son Too

Men also want to be pampered. You know his mother pampered him before. Now, it is your turn to pamper him. Whatever is negative word or action that you cannot tell or take on your first son or brother, don't tell or take on your husband. He is your first son before your first son. Remember he had been used to positive words and actions from his mother. He doesn't deserve anything less. He deserves to be treated like your first son or brother. The marriage will thrive and be robust if he finds the kind of love and care he used to have from his mother.

Capitalize on Second Chances

Marriage has its rough and tough times. It has a teething stage which both of you must carefully manage. Some people are not patient. They speak before they think. They act before they contemplate. They are quick to speak, quick to act and slow to hear.

The second half of every competitive sport is always the decider. Therefore, do not decide on the negative until you give yourselves a second chance. Have a second chance in your love affairs. Have a second chance in your trust boat. Have a second chance in your words, thought and action. Don't be irrational and illogical. Don't jump from A to Z. Don't start at 1 and jump to 100. Take things one step after the other and always leave room for adjustments. Second chance is the deepest. And second edition is usually better!

Have Three Instruments Handy

19

There are three words you must never leave out of your vocabulary. Those who don't have it in their dictionary always failed to sustain a great relationship. And those who have these words in abundance always managed to row the boat to a safe haven. The words are:

- I love you
- Thank you
- I am sorry

These are essential words that have no expiry date. They will work for you any time you want them to work. Some marriages have crumbled simply because he cannot say, *I love you.* What is difficult in saying these words over and over again? You lose nothing saying them and you gain a lot of her love and respect by saying them.

There are marriages that crashed for lack of expression of gratitude. It isn't that the person is not grateful but failure to express it is detrimental. The words *Thank you* conveys a lot of understanding. Not saying them makes you look like an ingrate. Saying them puts you in a vantage position to receive more. Now, what is difficult in saying thank you? Even if he will tell you not to mention, please mention it. It is detrimental if you don't. Even God frowns at us if we don't say THANK YOU!

And of course there are marriages that crumbled because *I am sorry* is not in the dictionary of either or both of the couple. This is a big one. God wants us to say sorry when we err. *I am sorry* does a lot of magic. I call it magical words. It can turn a furious person into a most amiable one. It can turn anger to laughter. It can prepare the bedroom for an exciting sport on the bed. It can open the wallet and release some wads. It can wipe out resentment in split seconds. Do you want to radicalize your marriage? Learn to say *I love you, I am sorry, Thank you.*

The Winning Combination: Love and Vision

20

Love contacts and introduces Marriage but in the long run, it is vision that sustains marriage. "Without vision the people perish". Equivocally, without vision, the marriage contract will perish! Any marriage without vision is hanging on a loose platform of endurance and possible disintegration.

How wonderful it will be that "friends" who want to get married sit down and have a lengthy discussion on what their marriage will look like forever. **VISION** will ensure that the **LOVE** relationship is first a Godly order and must be guided by guidelines outlined in God's book of life.

Marriage is not a short haul contract. It is a long haul, a life time journey. Intending couples must seek knowledge for everlasting marriage by establishing a viable and godly vision. The time of vision sharing is the best quality time any couple can ever have. People should not go to honeymoon to watch the moon. Couples who go to honey moon should return with honey in their mouths, having reviewed and consolidated the vision for their marriage.

Your vision should love and your love should consolidate your vision. Your vision should include raising your children in a Godly manner until you watch them bring up their own children in a Godly manner. Let this vision be fresh in your hearts after many years. Vision is the foundation upon which love exists. There are times, at later years when love begins to wane, vision will not let love perish. It will continue to provide its shoulders for the marriage to hang on until love bounces back. So, between love and vision, the winner is both!

Your Spouse is Gold

Every man's wife is gold to be mined, excavated, refined and processed before her shine can be obtained. As a man, it is your prerogative to excavate her. The truth is that every treasure that provides utility to man on earth has been hidden by God underneath the earth. This includes gold, diamond, iron, oil, etc. It is very expensive to excavate, mine and refine these natural endowments. It takes a lot of resources, expertise and patience.

Such is what is required of every husband in order to get the best from his wife. One of the instruments you need is patience. She is a gift from God. And this gift is intended to be productive. Every good and perfect gift of God that has a positive beginning is destined to have a positive ending. God never ends anything in the negative.

In order to radicalize your marriage, husbands exercise patience with errant wives so you can reap the benefit of "Gold at last!" God is expecting you to show love and manifest maturity. Don't quit the relationship. Some people are too quick to rush to separation and divorce. This should not be so. The 'good thing' in a wife can only be brought out by a good man who must be patient to endure, even under extreme provocation, to the end. Therefore, see to it that you endure to the end as husband or wife. Your marriage can become a reference point to save other marriages.

Between Power, Authority and Influence

> *'And God said, Let us make man in our image, after our likeness: and let them have dominion over the fish of the sea, and over the fowl of the air, and over the cattle, and over all the earth, and over every creeping thing that creepeth upon the earth. So God created man in his own image, in the image of God created he him; male and female created he them. And God blessed them, and God said unto them, Be fruitful, and multiply, and replenish the earth, and subdue it: and have dominion over the fish of the sea, and over the fowl of the air, and over every living thing that moveth upon the earth'* – Gen. 1:26-28

God created man and gave him power, authority and dominion. We can see this from the Scriptures. Adam was blessed and mandated to exercise dominion over all of God's creation. He is the head of God's creation. He is the head of the family. He has physical power much more than the weaker vessel. He has emotional strength. He is a rallying point and a symbol of authority. And he has something ego he protects from being trampled.

> *'And Adam gave names to all cattle, and to the fowl of the air, and to every beast of the field; but for Adam there was not found an help meet for him. And the LORD God caused a deep sleep to fall upon Adam and he slept: and he took one of his ribs, and closed up the flesh instead thereof; And the rib, which the LORD God had taken from man, made he a woman, and brought her unto the man. And Adam said, This is now bone of my bones, and flesh of my flesh: she shall*

be called Woman, because she was taken out of Man' – Gen. 2:20-23

We can see the demonstration of his power, authority and dominion. He gave name to all the animals in the Garden of Eden. And when his wife came out of him, he gave her a name: Woman. This creature called man is powerful! But there is something else. Power, authority and dominion alone cannot bring total progress. There is something more that when properly channeled, it leads to progress. This thing can control power, authority and dominion. What is this thing?

Influence! Ask Eve

Adam had power, authority and dominion but Eve had influence. Every man has power, authority and dominion. Every woman has influence. And the first principle in making **INFLUENCE** effective is positioning. Eve positioned herself **BY THE SIDE** of her husband and influenced him to eat the fruit that is in the center of the Garden.

If Eve stayed by the side of her husband and influenced him to the negative, you can stay by the side of your husband and **INFLUENCE** him to the positive. Positively or negatively, you cannot influence your spouse from a distance. Get close and stay side by side.

Remember that your husband is your first child before your first child. If your first child deviates from family norms, you can't separate from him or her. You will reverently sit him or her down and do some counseling. Do so with your husband. Men like to be treated as kindly as their mom treated them when they were growing. Influence your husband positively. Influence him to love God and be godly. Influence him to fast and pray. Influence him to take good and godly decisions. Eve used her influence negatively, use yours positively. Your marriage will be great!

Love is Key

24

The bible tells us that "love covers a multitude of sins." In my opinion, divorce uncovers a magnitude of sins. Love forgives. Love is kind and gentle. Love endures all things. Love is not selfish and proud. It is not easily provoked. Even when the common 'unforgiveable?' sin of 'he cheated on me or she cheated on me' surreptitiously creeps in to steal, kill and destroy like a thief, love rises up to the occasion and forgives.

When we fail to quickly reconcile a hurt in marital relationship, we open the door for long journey into the wilderness of separation and divorce. The devil sneaks in and whispers to their ears, *'Irreconcilable differences, Incompatibility.* This ultimately suggests the next step called separation or divorce. These words are the apt description of the character of the enemy of the peace of man – the devil, whose objective will remain to steal, to kill and to destroy. As occasion warrants, spouses should honor each other with reconciliation over little issues in the household. Let love rule and reign supreme. Joy and peace shall prevail afterwards.

Look Away or Look Aware

25

Marriage is an institution where offence cannot be excluded. If you cannot forgive or look away, you are not fit to marry. While you are seeking for a wife, have your two eyes open. They will be useful when you go shopping in preparation for the wedding ceremony. But after the ceremony and the couples get home, have one eye closed. The Bible says WATCH and PRAY. The opened eye is watching to find and fix errors while the closed eye **LOOKS** AWAY. This is how to 'Watch' and 'Pray'.

Do you have one of your eyes closed in your relationship? It is excellent to have your two eyes open when you are looking for a wife but once you have her, close one of your eyes. Overlook when necessary. The eye that is closed never sees her errors. The one that is open detects and fixes things without stirring the hornet's nest. It cleans the spilt milk, covers the pot, shuts the kitchen door, replaces water containers in the refrigerator, wipes the dusty television, places the remote control on the table, mops the wet floor, flushes the used toilet and fixes lots of things without making any fuss.

Are your two eyes open? You will certainly find faults in your spouse. Close one and open the other for the purpose of fixing the errors. Be your husband. Be your with your wife. Don't be easily irritated. Bear with her as unto the weaker vessel.

Forgive and Forgive

Unforgiveness in marriage is a cancer that has no immediate or prolonged remedy. The elimination or duration of cure is in the hand of spouses. A quick tempered wife who has no self-control can run her temper anywhere, anytime and at little provocation. Her husband must decorate himself with the garment of forgiveness if he wants to honor God with his marriage. The same goes for a short tempered man. He can set the whole house ablaze. To forgive, get a blotter or an eraser. Forgiveness is the reason pencils have erasers.

The pencil is made up of two sides. The outer layer made up of wood and the inner layer which houses the pencil itself. To write with pencil, the outer layer has to be sharpened by the user in order to get to the 'utility' part of the pencil. During usage, if there is a mistake in writing, the top side of the pencil bearing the eraser is brought to clean off the mistake, so writing could continue without ceasing.

A couple should be ready to use their erasers to erase things that challenge their peace. The essence of the pencil is 'continuity'. The pencil is like the generator switchgear. It does not give space for a delay in continuation of electrical communication. A house where switchgear is installed will always ensure that there is no breakdown in electricity. As soon as light is disrupted as result of one electrical fault or the other, the switchgear automatically switches on the stand-by generator as if nothing happened.

The problem with couples of the world is that they do not remember to apply the eraser when mistakes are made. Most people remember it when issues have gotten off hands and un-amendable. You can radicalize your marriage going forward by using the eraser. Your hugs, kisses and intimacy will rejuvenate your relationship.

Put on the garment of forgiveness 24/7 and make up your mind to forgive your spouse in advance of any kind of hurt. Simple acts can restore, re-fire and reignite freshness in the relationship. Remember, the enemy will always desire to sift your marriage. Both of you must make up your minds not to be sifted. Forgiveness is your weapon.

Trash the Offence

In each case of misunderstanding, there is the offence, offender and offended. The offended reacts against the offender in most cases, trashing him or her for the offence. Rather than trash the offender, trash the offence. This is the secret of successful marriages.

Every offender or offended is carrying a vision. You cannot stop the devil from attacking the vision. Vision is subject to attack by the enemy who adds two prefixes (di) before the vision and changes it to division. This is what the devil seeks to do in every marriage. Trash the offence and redeem the offender. By redeeming the offender, you will redeem the vision and make it continue to thrive.

Beware of the evil one behind the veil. When you see offence, the enemy is lurking around. He is not just after distorting your emotions but seeking to corrupt your love and vision. Remember, love and vision is like Siamese twin. If the enemy hurts one, the other is hurt too. So, close the door to the spirit of offence. Keep your love and vision thriving.

Be Alert

Be alert and beware. The devil is very patient. He lurks around like a stalker. The Bible describes him as 'like a roaring lion'. He is not a lion but he is 'like' a lion. Jesus is the Lion of the tribe of Judah.

> *'Be sober, be vigilant; because your adversary the devil, as a roaring lion, walketh about, seeking whom he may devour: Whom resist stedfast in the faith, knowing that the same afflictions are accomplished in your brethren that are in the world. But the God of all grace, who hath called us unto his eternal glory by Christ Jesus, after that ye have suffered a while, make you perfect, stablish, strengthen, settle you'* – 1 Peter 5:8-10

The devil is crafty as ever. He walks about like a roaring lion seeking whom to devour and he devours big when he has the opportunity. The word of God tells us to resist him and remain steadfast in the faith. The hordes of hell will never cease to unleash evil against the family but you have the power to protect and preserve yours. The grace of God is available for you to overcome all satanic attacks.

> *'Lest Satan should get an advantage of us: for we are not ignorant of his devices'*- 2 Cor. 2:11

Be alert and beware of the wiles of the devil. Don't let the devil take advantage over you to mess up your relationship by your petty anger or suspicion. If you are ignorant of his devices, he will play a fast one. Put on the whole armour of God so that you can resist the wiles, pranks and deceptions of the devil. Your marriage is a blessing, don't let it be cursed.

Hate What God Hates

Hate what God hates: divorce. God hates divorce! If you allow wisdom to lead you in your relationship, you will always win. Marriages fail largely because of lack of wisdom and understanding. When God brought Eve to Adam, He armed them with wisdom. That's why the marriage worked even after the great fall in the Garden of Eden. Do you think the marriage of Adam failed? Adam, the first man and Eve, the first lady had a successful marriage. Hold on a little bit as I explain better.

The serpent deceived Eve and Eve lured Adam to eat the fruit that God warned not to eat. They fell greatly together. And together they recovered greatly. They recovered from the attack of the devil and stayed together *till death do us part*. Their marriage was not **FOR BETTER I STAY, FOR WORSE I GO**. They gave birth to Cain and Abel. When another tragedy struck that Cain killed Abel, Adam and Eve got over the sorrow of loss and moved on happily. The generation of husbands and wives we have today would have handled these tragedies negatively.

1. Today's husband will label Eve a witch for luring him to eat the forbidden fruit.
2. The husband of this generation would have made the home a hopeless hell for Eve and constantly blame her for his misfortune.
3. The husband of today will put the information about Eve's greed for the forbidden fruit online and boost it to go viral.
4. Today's husband will make the interaction between Eve and the serpent to be all over the YouTube.
5. WhatsApp would be awash with this caption: *'How my wife caused me to disobey God'*.

6. Today's husband would explain his predicament via twitter: *'my wife disobeyed God, ate the apple and deceived me to partake of her disobedience'. Women are terrible!*

From the attitude of this great couple, you would agree with me that Adam and came out **stronger together** after the great fall. Divorce was not an option. They did not sink in their predicament. God was with them as in the beginning when they started the journey. May your home be a wonderful abode in Jesus name! May you stay stronger together in spite of what happens in Jesus name!

Watch Your Advisers

30

'Blessed is the man that walketh not in the counsel of the ungodly, nor standeth in the way of sinners, nor sitteth in the seat of the scornful' – Psalms 1:1

Watch your adversaries, they were once your advisers. You will do well to beware of your friends and draw your enemies close. It is the same as watching your advisers. They know so much about you that they can use against you. This is why you must beware of those you call friends and bring those that are fiends close enough for you to keep an eye on them.

'For their heart studieth destruction, and their lips talk of mischief' – Prov. 24:2

This is a company of people you must not keep: those whose heart seeks to destroy and whose lips talk mischief. The Message translation says: 'All they think about is causing a disturbance; all they talk about is making trouble'. There are people like that all around. When someone tells you to maltreat or even neglect your wife so that she will learn some lessons and respect you, beware of such person. His or her heart thinks destruction. His lips talk mischief. The Bible tells us how a man can gain the respect of his wife. Ephesians 5: 25 says: Husbands, love your wives even as Christ also love the Church and gave himself for it'. This is the Biblical way to gain respect and not physical or emotional assault. Anyone who counsels you to maltreat your wife in order to gain her respect is an evil person; an agent of darkness. Let us look at the amplified version of the Bible:

'For their mind plots oppression and devise violence and their lips talk of causing trouble and vexation'- Prov. 24:2

There are people whose mind plot oppression and devise violence. Their lips talk of causing trouble and vexation. They cause violence and oppression in relationships. They can end the relationship and be courageous to say I will marry another person. Avoid such kind of people. Marriage is not **FOR BETTER I STAY, FOR WORSE I GO.** Marriage is a **TOGETHER FOREVER** relationship. Never nurse an alternative plan to your relationship.

Better Reuniting Than Remarrying

31

Reunite, don't remarry. It is better to reunite than to remarry because remarrying brings with it 100% uncertainty. Leaving a known terrain to an unknown one is riskier. New level, new devil, that's what it is. Reconstruction in marriage is better than a new construction. A problem known is half solved. At least you know the causes of your frequent frictions. Sit together and resolve it than separating and remarrying another.

When relationship sours to the point where the husband or wife is thinking of quitting the marriage, it is the time to look at the vision, plan and purpose of God for marriage. It is the time for the husband to see his wife as an integral part of him. And it is the time for the wife to see the man as the rock from which she was hewn.

There are two major things God ordered man to 'seek.' One is the kingdom of God. The second is 'Peace'. He did not only order us to 'seek peace'. He commanded us to 'pursue peace'- The Bible says: Follow peace with all men, and holiness, without which no man shall see the Lord: Hebrews 12:14. The Amplified version says: Strive to live in peace with everybody and pursue that consecration and holiness without which no one will ever see the Lord.

Peace is the solid rock that sustains the structure of marital relationships. Husbands do not allow chaotic conditions in your home. Pursue peace at all cost.

Tell on Yourselves

Adam and Eve were naked and were not ashamed. They were transparent with each other. They excluded grudges and malice in their dispositions. They sat together to resolve issues rather than keep a catalogue of wrong doings in their finite mind. The Bible says we should be children in malice. You know it, children don't nurse grudges neither do they keep malice. God expects the husband and wife to be thus minded.

Tell on yourselves. Tell your partner when you are hurt rather than pretend that all is well. A nursed grudge is a viper in the bosom. Tell on yourselves when anything goes amiss and make sure you are abreast with each other. But be careful not to admit the blame game. A soft or gentle telling on yourselves will eliminate the semblance of blame game. The Bible says a soft answer turns away wrath.

Take It From Where You Left It

33

Marriage comes in chapters.

- Chapter one is when the man and woman are alone and unmarried. This is the stage a man draws a wish list, how he wants his wife to look like. The woman too fantasizes how her husband should look like.
- Chapter two is when God connects them together. The man finds the will of God for him, she also discovers the right man for her.
- Chapter three is when the nuptial cord is tied and the newlyweds go on honey moon to discover more love.
- Chapter four is when they return from honey moon to live together as husband and wife. This is when the real marriage journey begins.
- Chapter five is when children start to come as blessings of marriage.

Where did you leave your marriage? At the reception table or in the moon? Then take the marriage and drop the wedding. Take the honey and drop the moon. Some people live their marriage at the reception table while others leave it in the moon. There are those who leave it in the labour room. Soon after delivery and babies come, they shift attention completely to the fruits. Take back your marriage where you left it.

Your Choice in Marriage Determines the Course of Your Life

34

Look before you leap. This is very true in marriage contract. Good choice will lead to good end and bad choice will lead to bad end. Your choice determines the course of your life. Whether you will succeed or fail in life largely depends on your choice of marriage partner. A young man barely made both ends meet before he married. Shortly after he married, things turned around for him drastically. He experienced rapid success financially and spiritually. Within a few years, he built houses, expanded his business and established new ones. Another man was doing well before he married. Few years into the marriage, his business began to decline until he was bankrupt. Your choice of spouse largely determines your destiny. So, **look before you leap**.

> *'I will instruct thee and teach thee in the way which thou shalt go: I will guide thee with mine eye'* – Psalms 32:8

God will instruct and teach us how to go about our marriage. The onus is with you to be sensitive and responsive to His guidance. As the shepherd of our souls, we must listen and follow instructions. He will never lead us astray.

Behaviour Before Beauty

It is one thing to be beautiful and another to have good character. What's the point marrying a beautiful damsel who is character deficient? Some people marry for beauty. They make their choice on the premise of appearance. This is why when beauty fades away like the flower of the fields in drought, the foundation crumbles. If I have to choose between beauty and behaviour, I will pick the latter.

Some people do not care so long as the damsel is beautiful. They marry beauty without good behaviour. The best beauty should be good behaviour. Some people marry beauty without brains. Later in the journey, they will discover that beauty is not enough to contract marriage.

When behaviour; attitude or character is in, beauty is in. **Beauty without behaviour is a disaster that will be full blown someday.** When it happens, it becomes too late to make amends. Behaviour should be placed well ahead beauty. **Moreover, good behaviour is beautiful!**

Marriage is Made in Heaven; It is only Celebrated on Earth

36

Most people consider only the earthly celebration: the groom's suit, the bride's gown, the dance steps, the reception, accolades, gifts, etc. They do not consider where marriage is made. For you to have a great marriage, you need to **look up** before you **hook up** with him or her or him. What's the fuss about celebration when the source of marriage is neglected? Brethren, good marriages come from Heaven. Marriages can be made in hell too. It depends on where you picked your partner. If the devil gives you his daughter, he becomes your in-law. Never allow satan's gift. Young girl, refuse the enemy's gift of a suitor. You can have a godly man made in heaven. You can have a beautiful and godly woman made in heaven.

The choice is exclusively yours! Go for heaven made damsel. Beloved sister, go for heaven made groom. This will make your marriage enjoyable. Marriage should be enjoyed and not endured. Look up also if you didn't before you hooked up. It is never too late to do so.

The Bible enjoins us to look up unto the hills from where comes our help

Wedding Lasts But for a Day, Marriage Continues 'Till Death Do Us Part'

37

All of the ceremonies and activities that come with wedding do not really last. They all vanish with the wedding day. After wedding, marriage begins and continues till *death do us part*. You will be wise therefore to give priority to what is sustainable. Give more attention to your marriage rather than the wedding. Have a good wedding but also have a great marriage. Spend money to organize your wedding but be willing and ready to spend twice as much to maintain your marriage.

Some people had a great wedding but ended up having a bad marriage. This is pathetic. It is better to have a bad wedding but a great marriage than to have a great wedding and bad marriage. Marriage is the main thing and not wedding. As much as you plan your wedding, please plan your marriage. Give it a hundred percent attention. God bless you!

Bad Marriage is a Living Hell

38

The next worse thing after hell fire is a bad marriage. In fact, bad marriage is a living hell. You know what it is when you place a cat and dog in the same pen. A young man married only to find himself in the den of a lioness. She could talk from dusk till dawn like parrot, nagging and bragging. When the husband stands up to leave the house in order to douse tension, she would grab and physically assault him. It was a constant practice. When he couldn't bear her any longer, he walked away from the marriage. His home was a living hell. You must patiently make the right choice as the Lord guides you. Marrying wrongly is disastrous.

A godly damsel married a young handsome man once upon a time. Their wedding was the talk of the town. It was well attended and celebrated. A month into the marriage, she discovered the beast in the handsome man. He would beat her at the slightest provocation. His physical assault became unbearable after repeated bashing and battery until she invited a divorce lawyer. That was how the marriage collapsed. Bad marriage is a living hell.

Marry for the Right Reason

39

When you blindly get married, you will openly see the reality someday. It takes marriage to open the blind eyes of love. When the marriage wine runs out, the rest is history because the eyes will be wide open to reality. Couples either commit suicide, homicide or sue for divorce.

To some people, marriage wine is the money. Some ladies blindly marry a man because of money. When money runs out, '*for better for worse till death do us part* will become '*for better I stay... for worse I go*'. To others, the marriage wine is the shape and curves of the damsel. Some men marry a woman because of outward structure. After one or two births and when the shape changes from a slender looking damsel to a fat mother, love gets sick. In this case, it is genuine love that will keep the marriage. Don't be led blindly to love and marry. Have a genuine love; unconditional love; the kind of love that will stand the heat of trials and temptations. When you marry for the right reason, your marriage will prosper. You will wax stronger and stronger in love.

It is Better for People to Laugh at you for Marrying Late yhan for them to be Unable to Laugh With You After Marriage

40

There is no laughter in some homes. Everything is topsy-turvy. There is no love, peace or joy. The home is a demonic stronghold. May you not hastily marry the wrong person and live in remorse all your life. When you marry correctly, even though late, you will have a prosperous marriage. People will laugh with you eventually even though they laughed at you before. He that laughs last laughs best.

Let people continue to laugh at you for not getting married now, they will laugh with you later. It is better for them to laugh **AT** you now and laugh **WITH** you later than for nobody to be available to laugh with you as a result of hasty and disastrous marriage.

Marriage Can Be a Holy Wedlock or Unholy Deadlock

41

Which one do you want, the former or the latter? The choice is exclusively yours! It largely depends on your attitudes and dispositions. Do you want your marriage to work and be a holy wedlock? Then, do everything to be progressive. Play your part diligently. Love, care, be considerate and tolerant. Avoid the rough and thorny paths of blame game and carefree attitude of w-h-a-t-e-v-e-r! Don't be cynical or sarcastic. Put in every positive effort to make things work out well between you and your spouse. Don't get boxed to the corner that leads to deadlock. You can navigate through the vicissitudes of the marriage lane and emerge victorious. Agree rather than argue. Consider rather than being inconsiderate. Tolerate rather than being intolerant. Let the opinion of each other count. Give room for compromise. Don't always stand on your opinion. Give in when it is not harmful to the relationship. Moreover, let your disagreements be brought under the searchlight of prayer. You will succeed to remove the thorn amongst the bed of roses.

Successful Marriage is Always a Triangle

42

God at the top and the couple at the base. When God is not at the top, your guess is right, the devil will hastily occupy the vacuum. And when the devil is at the top of the triangle, the marriage ship will capsize sooner or later. What is (will be) the composition of your marriage? Is God at the Top? Will God be at the top? Make sure God is at the top of the triangle. Your marriage will certainly be successful.

Pray together upon waking up from sleep and pray together when you retire to sleep. Share the word of God constantly. Fast and pray when you are inspired to. Be actively involved in ministry. Don't be an idle mind in the church. Play a role. Do something. Let God be your first and last resort. When God is in, the devil is out!

Everything God Made was Good According to Scriptures. There was Only One Thing that waas Not Good: Man Without Woman

43

'And the LORD God said, It is not good that the man should be alone; I will make him an help meet for him' – Gen. 2:18.

God saw that it is not good for Adam to be alone even though he was going about his business in the Garden of Eden. Adam didn't have the slightest thought of a companion. God saw the emptiness and filled it by providing Eve. Has God filled your loneliness? If yes, congratulations. If no, please, wait patiently for Him to do so. He will guide you perfectly.

Don't be alone. The Bible says two are better than one. It also says one shall chase a thousand and two shall chase ten thousands. What is not good is not good. It is not good to be alone. Seek godly companionship. May the Lord guide you.

What is the Pin Number of Your Spouse?

44

Pin numbers gives you access to your electronic or digital devices like androids, tablets, iPhones, computer, etc. Without it, your access will be limited. Do you have what you do to make your spouse open up? When your relationship is threatened, do you have what it takes to revitalize it? If you have the PIN number of your spouse, you can always win him or her over. You can save the day. PIN numbers vary:

John Bello, my editor in Nigeria and his amiable wife, Sarah have their PIN numbers. A PIN number is a melting point. It doesn't matter the weight of acrimony, and it doesn't matter who stirred the hornet's nest, John would usually buy Sarah a gift on his way from office. Rather than get upset with her, he would put the gift in her hand upon opening the door to the bedroom. Sarah has her joker too. She usually would say, *'shall we pray'* when it is bedtime. That always ended any rancor. It is always easy to talk things through after either card (John's gift or Sarah's *'shall we pray'*) is placed on the table.

Copulate Regularly

Sex is good and pleasurable. It is an intimate activity designed to be practiced and enjoyed within the bounds of marriage. It is a strong emotion, second only to hunger. Sex is sweet! It brings joy and refreshment. It soothes the mind and emotion of participants. It is therapeutic. More sex means more bonding.

Some men are very active in the living room with soccer. They can spend several hours watching football. Some women are very active too in the kitchen. The bedroom should be much more active for both of you. Spend quality time together. No hit and run business. Slow down and spend time with foreplay. Be romantic with words. Eye to eye contact will enhance more bonding. Do not be wanting in the bedroom. Whatever is the matter, let the '**bedmeeting**' game outshine the **badminton** racket game. Amen!

Don't deny your spouse his or her conjugal right. Misunderstanding should have nothing to do in the bedroom. Finish your fights when you get down on the bed. God is watching to applaud you for this sense of responsibility.

Argue to Agree

46

There is room for argument but always agree afterwards. Sometimes, arguments and quarrels could be healthy. You are the one who can make it so. If you position yourself well, arguments and quarrels are like intimacy. Sometimes, you need them to consolidate. You know, our parents quarreled at the farm land and returned to give birth to us.

Give room for the opinions of each other. No man is an island. No man is a compendium of knowledge. Let your spouse explain his or her perspective. Something good could come out of it. God speaks to us in diverse ways. A little here, a little there and the best decision is reached. Quarrel and agree if you must but agree in conclusion.

Abort to Stay Healthy

Abortion is good. So, abort misunderstandings. Seek clarification. How often have we misjudged and torn each other to shreds with harsh words and actions before we have time to evaluate the situation? Presuming things our way without taking the time to find out exactly what the situation really is, we are quick to act and react. We take decisions based on poor judgment and regret afterwards.

Little patience can drastically reduce major life long mistakes. Yes, little patience can afford you to have more valuable and valid information that may alter your belief and decision. Little patience can open your eyes to the truth! Most problems are caused by lack of understanding or misunderstanding. With adequate understanding, there will be no issue you cannot resolve but if there is lack of understanding, you will fight on everything, no matter how insignificant.

In some relationships, little things have degenerated to a dismal end because of misunderstanding. Your lack of understanding can overwhelm your partner who has understanding if you are adamant. But if you lack understanding and humble to compromise, the understanding of your partner can overwhelm your lack of it and there will be meaningful progress. See to it that your misunderstandings are aborted quickly.

Be Man Enough

Marriage is not for boys. It is a serious business for men only. So, before marriage, be man. There are too many boys who walk down the aisles to the altar to tie the nuptial cord. This is why divorce is rampant. It is very appropriate to be grown up before you get engaged in marriage. Be man before marriage.

> 'When I was a child, I spake as a child, I understood as a child, I thought as a child: but when I became a man, I put away childish things' – 1 Cor. 13:11

Putting a round peg in a square hole will amount to failure. Doing fist what you should do last will amount to frustration in your relationships. Apostle Paul said, when I was a child, I spake as a child, I understood as a child, I thought as a child. Many adults behave like a child in their relationships. In fact, many adults are children in the real sense. How does a child behave?

1. First, a child speaks
2. Second, he tries to understand what he has spoken
3. Third, he now begins to think about what he has spoken.

The attitude of a mature person is exactly opposite. A mature person will not speak, understand and think. This is the correct order:

1. First, think
2. Second, understand
3. Third, speak

This attitude of thinking, understanding and speaking is very vital to healthy relationships. That is why you must be man before marriage. You were once a child but no more when you get married. In case you are not yet married, be man before you do. It will save you a lot of troubles!

Name Yourselves

49

'And out of the ground the LORD God formed every beast of the field, and every fowl of the air; and brought them unto Adam to see what he would call them: and whatsoever Adam called every living creature, that was the name thereof' – Gen. 2:19

Adam had the prerogative to name all the animals in the Garden of Eden. He also called his wife woman. The Bible says God endorsed his naming ceremony. Whatever he called the animals was approved. You are going to name your children someday but before that happens, name yourselves.

'And whatsoever Adam called every living creature, that was the name thereof'. Beware, your word has power. Whatever you call yourselves shall be sanctioned. It shall receive God's approval. Be positive in your approach. Call yourselves what you want to see. For example, call yourselves 'Blessed' and you will see blessings in abundance. Call yourselves 'Miracle' and your marriage will experience miracles all the way. Call yourselves love, peace, joy, grace, greatness, etc and it will happen accordingly. There is power in your tongue, so use it judiciously. God bless you.

Keep Your Matrimony Holy

50

There are three HOLY prefixes: Holy Bible, Holy Spirit and Holy Matrimony. Keep your matrimony holy. Don't be the heathen, your marriage is not. It is called Holy Matrimony. Marriage is honourable. It began in the Garden of Eden and God was the moderator. There is a world of difference between a heathen marriage and holy matrimony. You cannot run your marriage like the heathen. There are Biblical standards you must follow. Respect your marital vow.

In the course of your relationship, there could be challenges. Don't seek answers from the heathen. Blessed is the man who walks not in the counsel of the ungodly, stand in the way of sinners or sit on the seat of the scornful. Go back to the originator of marriage for answers. There is no problem too difficult to be resolved. No question too hard to be answered and no nut too hard to crack. You will win if you look up. So, look up and hook up!

Serve and Follow

Seek to serve and not only to be served. Marriage is a huge project. There are different department in this everlasting project. The kitchen department is one. The laundry department is another. There is the sowing and birthing department in the bedroom. There is also the financial department as there is cleaning department. The bottom line is service. Serve, serve and serve. It is never too much to serve the one you love dearly.

Render your service to make breakfast, lunch and dinner. While one person is fixing breakfast, the other is cleaning the house. While one is serving in the laundry department, the other is fixing dinner. Don't wait for the jack of all trades. Marriage is not a master-servant relationship. We are co-heirs or joint-heirs together in Christ. There is nothing like my money. It is our money. We are both winners: bread winners, blessing winners, heaven winners and winners all the way.

We have our prime example in Christ Jesus. Though Lord and Master, He stooped down to wash the feet of His disciples. Though the Bridegroom, He served the Bride. Let us follow His steps. Let us serve one another in humility and love. We shall be the greatest when we stoop down to be the least. Marriage is sweetest when we try to outdo one another in service. Amen.

What Do You Want From Me?

52

Elisha served Elijah to full capacity. First, he gave up his business to follow his master. He served diligently until the divine call that would take away his master was imminent. Yet, he followed him very closely from Gilgal to Bethel, Jericho and Jordan. At this peak of followership, Elijah said to him: 'Ask what I shall do for thee, before I be taken away from thee'. Elijah gave Elisha this golden opportunity only after the latter had served him sincerely. He received the exact thing he asked for.

Serve him until he asks you: 'What do you want from me?' Serve him sincerely and to his satisfaction. Serve him his favorite meals. Serve him with respect and honor. Serve him in the bedroom satisfactorily. Serve Him with what will make him happy and joyful. Serve him with peace.

Serve her until she asks you: 'What do you want from me?' Serve her to her satisfaction. Serve her by lavishing your love on her. Serve her with TLC, tender loving care. Serve her in the bedroom until she is satisfied. Serve her with peace and joy. Serve her with the assurance of security.

Marriage is sweet when you serve each other. Use this nugget and key regularly and you will see the wonder that will happen. Your marriage will experience a glow of progress. Both of you will be happy and your relationship will be healthy forever.

Take Your Wife to Canaan

53

Canaan is the land of promise. It is the land that flows with milk and honey; a land of prosperity and prospect; a wealthy land. Take your wife to this Promised Land. Take her to the land of peace and joy. Take her to a place where she feels secured.

> *'Thou shalt increase my greatness, and comfort me on every side'* – Psalms 71:21

She needs greatness and comfort on every side. She wants the best for her children. Take her to the place of greatness and all-round comfort. Make efforts as much as you can to achieve this Canaan experience. Let her dreams be fulfilled. Let her joy be full. The Bible says in Jeremiah 29:11, 'For I know the thoughts that I think toward you, saith the LORD, thoughts of peace, and not of evil, to give you an expected end'. Make this happen for her by your prayer, love and sacrifice.

Take Your Wife and Children to Goshen

54

The land of Goshen is named in the Bible as the place in Egypt given to the Hebrews by the Pharaoh of Joseph and the land from which they later left Egypt at the time of the Exodus. It was located in the eastern Delta of the Nile. Goshen means a land of plenty and comfort.

Take your wife to Goshen; the realm of plenty and comfort. Marriage is meant to be enjoyed, several people merely endure. Every woman needs comfort, security and plenty to enjoy. Your wife deserves this Goshen treat. Labour hard to provide enough for her comfort. Let her not lack anything good. God provided the niceties of life in the Garden of Eden. You too as a little god in your family should make adequate provision. Preserve, project, protect and provide for her. It is your responsibility.

Your children deserve to enjoy the niceties of life. As you curdle your wife on the right, curdle your children on the left. They should enjoy the best your marriage is designed to offer. Take them to the realm of plenty and comfort. Let them be proud of the parents they have. They will honor you and learn to outdo your legacy.

Understanding is Vital

55

One is weak, the other is weaker. When the Bible calls the woman a weaker vessel, it means there is a weak vessel. In the superlative degree, it is thus arranged: Weak, Weaker and Weakest. The man is weak, the woman is weaker and the infants are weakest. In order to revolutionize your marriage and make it positive, you will do well to be the weakest for each other. Understanding is the key. Understanding is going under each other to stand.

> *'Likewise, ye husbands, dwell with them according to knowledge, giving honour unto the wife, as unto the weaker vessel, and as being heirs together of the grace of life; that your prayers be not hindered'*- 1 Peter 3:7

Relate with your spouse by going under each other to stand. This is the new definition of understanding. Dwell peaceably according to knowledge. Understand each other so well. Understand her feminine make up. Understand his masculine make up. Don't expect her to behave like HIM and don't expect him to behave like HER. There two different make up here. Understand each other in this perspective. To the man especially, if you don't understand and give her honour, your prayers will be hindered. The Bible says so!

Watch It!

Don't invite dogs to daggle and rats to rattle around you. This is what leads to divorce! Be careful not to allow space or gaps between you. Block every little crack in the wall of your marriage. It is little foxes that are allowed to fester that destroy the vine. No matter is too trivial to be looked into and resolved. If you allow it to fester, it will degenerate to a bigger issue that will become very difficult to handle.

Find out what upsets her. Know what puts him off. These are the dogs and rats you must not allow to daggle and rattle around you. They come in between you to create a gap. Watch it and close the gap. Don't let them distract you from your love. Focus on her always. Let him not far out of reach. Let your togetherness be sacrosanct. You are meant for each other. So stay close to each other always.

Don't Blow Your Cover

57

It is better to stay married and be naked in holiness. Don't be separated by blowing your cover. Adam and Eve stayed together. The Bible says they were both naked and were not ashamed. They didn't allow themselves to be daggled or rattled.

Some couples easily blow off their cover and rush to the divorce lawyer over a little misunderstanding. Adam and Eve had misunderstandings too but they didn't blow their cover. They stayed married in spite of all odds. They had knowledge for everlasting marriage.

Your spouse is your covering; don't blow off the covering by separation. Removing the covering will make you naked and ashamed unlike in the Garden when they were both naked and not ashamed. They were naked yet covered. Their covering was each other's trust and integrity. Their covering was their love, service and submission to each other. With this covering, the divorce lawyer is useless and jobless.

Do you have your covering intact? Please keep it intact so that the divorce lawyer will file up for another kind of job instead of jumping at offers that aid separation. Be one another's keeper. Keep everything keep able: love, trust, kindness, submission, humility, patience, understanding, etc. Stay married! Stay covered!

Love Like a Dog

Dogs love human beings unconditionally and sacrificially. The dog is stubborn in its desire to protect human beings yet sweet tempered when it comes to serving human beings. It sometimes stacks and chases on a regular basis. Confident, dominant, protective, independent and tolerant, the dog has the ability to work well with humans.

Love her like a dog loves its owner. From a very far distance, the dog can pick the home coming of its owner. It is accustomed to his or her smell. With celebration, the dog will welcome its owner each time. Welcome your spouse with a kiss. Celebrate his or her coming each time. Love unconditionally and sacrificially. Be confident, dominant, protective and tolerant in your love. Let the dogs teach you how to love out love from your lover.

Master Anger

One letter short of Danger, anger is a viper in the bosom. It seethes and lurks in the bosom of fools. Anger is a form of insanity in which the angry partner thinks of securing himself or herself with negative actions or words that will linger in the heart of the other party for some time. Rather than calm situations, anger makes it worse.

Anger triggers devastating capacity such as jealousy, wickedness, evil thoughts, hostile words, hate, impatience and more. One of the major tools the devil uses to create discord in marital relationship is anger. When anger brews, it is difficult for the spouse to ever sit down together to discuss. It gives one of them the uncanny ability to suddenly talk quicker, louder and more vociferously than the other, so much that the other person will not be prepared to listen again.

The Bible admonishes us to be slow to wrath. Anger can be quickly generic. It is a vice that parents can easily pass on to children from generation to generation. In most cases, anger is judgmental leaving no room for Grace and Mercy. Nobody benefits from the devastating aftermath of anger.

> *'Be ye angry, and sin not: let not the sun go down upon your wrath: Neither give place to the devil'* – Eph. 4:26-27

> *'Wherefore, my beloved brethren, let every man be swift to hear, slow to speak, slow to wrath'* – James 1:19

Be in control of your emotions. Don't be mad at each other, be rather mad together against anti-marriage forces. Cain killed his brother, Abel in anger. When you are angry, do something positive. Your positive action or reaction will remove the letter D in danger and replace the last letter

R with letter L. Danger minus D and R plus L is ANGEL. You can turn moments of anger into angelic moments. This happens when you act or react positively instead of negatively.   Anger can be put under control. It is your prerogative to do so. Calm down, down and down! Don't be in a hurry to speak. Hasty decisions during moments of anger will always portend danger. Master anger, don't let it master you.

Build Together

60

Marriage is like a tower. It must be built together, brick by brick. Remember the tower of Babel? The people maintained that togetherness that gave them the impetus to build day after day. God acknowledged their unity and vision to build the tower:

> 'And the LORD said, Behold, the people is one, and they have all one language; and this they begin to do: and now nothing will be restrained from them, which they have imagined to do' – Genesis 11:6

The first thing God noticed about the people was the togetherness. They were united towards one purpose. Because of this, God concluded that nothing will stop them from achieving their goal. Bring this vision, passion and unity together in marriage. Build by laying block upon block. Build together with passion brick by brick; a little here and there.

> 'Every wise woman buildeth her house: but the foolish plucketh it down with her hands' – Prov. 14:1

Build day by day by laying one block after the other. Build together by speaking positive words Build together by showering love, respect and submission one to another. Build together by exhibiting the fruit of the Spirit. Some people foolishly pluck down their marriage by their irrational actions and reactions. You can build together rather than destroy. Make intentional efforts to raise up your marriage rather than run it down carelessly as some people do. As you build together, so shall you enjoy peace, love and joy together in your home. Amen!

Worship Your Spouse Absolutely

The Bible tells us that there is only one true living God. This is true. We are required to worship God with all our heart, mind and soul. He is the only OBJECT of worship. Worshiping any other man made God is counted as idolatry. This is a punishable offence.

There is another form of worship you must do if you want to radicalize your marriage and make it positive. Worship your spouse with all of your body! God deserves your heart, mind and soul worship. Your spouse deserves your body worship. Give it to him any how! Give it her as she likes it! Worship each other as much as it is convenient. Worship each other wherever you can: the bedroom, living room, kitchen, bathroom or any other room!

Your object of worship is always one. No other God besides the God of Heaven and earth. No other body besides your spouse. Admire each other. Cherish each other's body. Care for it' caress it; invest your money to maintain it; keep it clean and alluring always. You have no other body to worship, so give it all you have!

Sow Good and Viable Seeds

62

Seeds sown will certainly germinate, grow to maturity and bring forth fruits in due season. Therefore, sow good and viable seeds. You will reap it in due season. If you sow the wind, you will reap the whirlwind. Harvest is usually greater.

You are allowed to be your own actor and actress in the theatre of your own bedroom. Therefore, use your sensuality to worship your one and only spouse in obedience to God. Keep in mind that while you are with your spouse, you are sowing seeds that both of you will remember. Both good and evil have their pay masters. If you sow bad seeds, you will have memory of it but always allow the memory of the good and right seeds sown bring you back together again and again. Let your coming together always be a time of refreshing!

Seek Unity Above All

63

I have talked about the fact that reuniting is better than remarrying. If you are not united, you will be disunited. Disunity breeds the seed of divorce. And when divorce occurs, there will be plenty of loneliness. One of the deadliest things divorce causes is emotional loneliness. You can be in the midst of people and still feel lonely. Only marriage can legitimately cure this kind of loneliness.

Loneliness is the pathway to all sorts of temptations. An idle mind is the devil's workshop. A lonely mind will be bombarded by demonic suggestions. Illicit sex will soon begin. It has been said that there is no satisfaction in illicit sex. The Bible says marriage is honorable. Sex within the ambits of marriage is therefore honorable. Illicit sex is dishonorable and brings shame afterwards.

Loneliness breeds seeds of illicit drugs. When illicit drugs set in, withdrawal begins and addiction results. Look at the many troubles of disunity. From disunity to divorce, illicit sex, illicit drugs, withdrawal and addiction. The trend is not complete yet. The voice that suggested divorce up to the point of addiction to illicit sex and drugs will soon suggest suicide to end it all. Why will someone go through all of these when unity is all you need to lead a happy and successful marriage? Therefore, seek unity always. Never allow the voice of discord. The devil is always lurking around to lend his voice of disunity. He is desperate to divide and spoil. Don't give him a place in your home!

The 80% Advantage of Reuniting

64

There is no marriage that is challenge-free. Just like it is on our motor roads, there are turns, bends, corners and roundabouts. Every problem has an equivalent of prospect. There is solution where problems exist. Now, reuniting comes with a huge advantage. Reuniting solves 80% of known problems. At least, the couples know what the problems are and why they fell apart. Now, reuniting brings to the table 80% advantage of success. They must have known what not to do to erode peace, love and joy. They must have known what to do to enhance love, peace and joy.

If you score 80% in an examination, you will coast home with victory. The other 20% of unknown will be resolved when the 80% solution is secured. All I am driving at is that reuniting is much better than looking for another spouse. There is always inexplicable joy of reunion. Reunite and set your marriage on fire with passionate love! Go now, your partner is waiting for you!

The 100% of Disadvantage in Remarrying

Have you heard of the saying: from frying pan to fire? Many marriages that hit the rocks have always been better than the new one. Remarrying is like an athlete running towards the finish line that suddenly drops the baton and returns to the start line. He starts all over again when he should have continued to the finish line. Perhaps, he has conquered more than 50% of the long haul. Now, he is about to start all over again.

Remarrying comes with the disadvantage of 100% unknown issues. It will be a lot easier for a medical student who is in the third year of his seven years medical school to continue to the fourth year and finish up at the seventh year than for that student to retire and start from year one in mechanical engineering school. He is a lot familiar with the medical jargons. He is acquainted with the terms and conditions associated with medicine. Now, in a new school, he just begins to learn again. He has 100% issues to learn and solve in his new school. This is what remarrying causes. There are many reversals to make. You will be better off reuniting than remarrying. Take that step today. Pick up your phone and kick start the process. Send an email to this effect. Make that move now!

You Can Go Back to Continue

66

Go back and continue from where you stopped. There is so much trouble in quitting and staying alone. You will soon let down your guards to illicit sex and drugs. There is also so much trouble remarrying for it comes with 100% of unknown issues. What shall we do then? Listen to the good voice of the author of marriage.

God does not abandon His people. He speaks to us for our good. The divorcee is always hearing God speak: 'you can go back, do not fear, for I am with you'. Dearly beloved of the Lord, believe in me, I am here for you also'. You will hear two different voices. One says, you can go back for I am with you. This is the voice of God. This is the advice I am giving here too. The other voice says, 'don't go back, you can satisfy your sexual desires with another'. This is a wicked voice that seeks to eventually destroy you. Be wise, close your ears to this carnal suggestion. It is only a carnal mind that will take heed of this carnal suggestion.

Revolutionize your marriage beginning from today! Go back and continue from where you left off. Go back and love her. Go back and submit to him. Let the fire glow again as in the days of courtship. Relive the memory of those romantic days. Your marriage can be rejuvenated. You can revive and grow it passionately. Yes, it can be better. Though your beginning was little, the end shall greatly increase. Better is the end of a thing than its beginning. You can achieve better results now if only you go back and continue from where you left off!

Obedience is Key

67

Moses demonstrated the power of God principally because he was obedient. Two scriptures readily come to mind when obedience is a subject of discourse:

> *'If ye be willing and obedient, ye shall eat the good of the land'* – Isa. 1:19

> *'If they obey and serve him, they shall spend their days in prosperity, and their years in pleasures. But if they obey not, they shall perish by the sword, and they shall die without knowledge'* – Job 36:11-12

Moses did exactly what he heard from God. Miracles upon miracles left Pharaoh and his magicians utterly startled. They admitted that it is the Finger of God at work! The rod of Moses was the token of signs and wonders. At every obedience, Moses witnessed miracles, signs and wonders.

Marriage is like the rod of Moses. Unless you throw the rod down in obedience and humility, you cannot experience its worth and miracles. Throwing the rod down in obedience is submitting your marriage to Biblical injunctions and instructions. If you are willing and obedient, you will eat the fruit of marriage. You will reap love, peace and joy. You will reap the fruit of the womb and raise a lovely family. You will enjoy great companionship and emotional stability.

The Bible enjoins the husband to love his wife as Christ loved the Church. Obey this instruction. Love is patient, selfless, kind and tolerant. Love is sacrificial and unconditional. The Bible also enjoins the wife to respect and submit to her husband. Obey this instruction. Obedience in this regard will birth miracles and blessings in the marriage. It will be like Moses experiencing new miracles each time he cast down his rod in obedience to instruction.

Avoid Book Keeping

68

Book keeping is the process of keeping records of daily transactions in business. A bookkeeper is hired to keep an accurate account of day to day transactions of the business or concern. The purpose is to ensure that all information and records necessary to balance the books of accounts to the satisfaction of the bookkeeper and owners of the company are diligently kept for future reference.

Bookkeeping is very good for commerce. It provides comprehensive information which enhances appraisal and decision making. As good as this is, bookkeeping is not a good word in Marriage. Spouses that keep records will always have exhaustless issues and challenges to quarrel about. The greatest problem of a relationship where grudges and wrong doings are saved in the mind's book is that no issue is ever too old to be brought up again.

Avoid keeping records of wrongs as much as you can. When records of wrongs are kept, problems long settled are brought up as often and as many times as the memory book of records is opened by any of the partners. Once kept, the records are remembered and re-enacted on daily, weekly, monthly and yearly basis. It is a very simple and sure way to sustain negative suspense in the family and spread unhappiness within and without the household.

When issues are resolved, delete them from your mental hard disk. Throw them into the sea of forgetfulness. Forgive and forget. Don't dig out what has been buried. Let bygone be bygone.

Entry Only

69

There is a Church that has this slogan: No exit, only entry. Their goal is to make sure everyone that enters the church is properly discipled, giving no room for the person to stop coming to Church. I think this slogan is very appropriate for the marriage institution. There should be no exit door.

In your marriage have only one door: the entry door. Make no provision for an exit door. The exit door in marriage is what people use to approach the divorce lawyer for separation and divorce. Close this door permanently. In fact, from the beginning, make no provision for this door. Enter and never come out of it. Enter to succeed at all cost. Burn your bridges behind you and never think of backing out.

Those who create the exit door sooner or later find reasons to back out. They find reasons to escape into the arms of another man or woman. They have plan B already mapped out while they are in marriage. It is as though they want to fail so that they can explore the plan B. This should not be so. Enter into marriage to succeed. Enter to fulfill the eternal purpose of God. Enter to glorify God and fulfill destiny.

She is Also Your Sister

70

'And Abraham journeyed from thence toward the south country, and dwelled between Kadesh and Shur, and sojourned in Gerar. And Abraham said of Sarah his wife, She is my sister: and Abimelech king of Gerar sent, and took Sarah. But God came to Abimelech in a dream by night, and said to him, Behold, thou art but a dead man, for the woman which thou hast taken; for she is a man's wife. But Abimelech had not come near her: and he said, Lord, wilt thou slay also a righteous nation? Said he not unto me, She is my sister? and she, even she herself said, He is my brother: in the integrity of my heart and innocence of my hands have I done this. And God said unto him in a dream, Yea, I know that thou didst this in the integrity of thy heart; for I also withheld thee from sinning against me: therefore suffered I thee not to touch her' – Gen. 20:1-6

Abraham referred to Sarah as his sister when king Abimelech asked about her. Though he said so out of fear, your wife is also your sister. She is your sister returned. So, treat her the way you treated your sister in your family of orientation. You certainly were protective of her. You made sure no man harassed her. You kept your eyes on her from time to time. You helped her with physical works. In fact, you had a soft for her in your heart!

You have left your family of orientation to start a family of procreation. You have left your siblings to cleave to another woman. That woman is your sister returned. Protect her like you used to do. Have a soft spot for her. Take care of her and shield her from any form of embarrassment. Remember she is truly your sister as both of you are heirs of salvation together. You belong to one Father which art in heaven!

Tame Your Tongue

71

In order to lead a blissful marriage, you must resolve to tame your tongue. Be swift to hear but slow to speak. Refrain from saying things you don't mean. And have the right choice of words when you do speak. The tongue is like a serpent that lies serene and quiet in the mouth as if it is harmless. But when it sticks out and pours out its venom, the victim will normally suffer from the poison while it retires quietly into the comfort of the mouth, unhurt and unharmed.

> 'For in many things we offend all. If any man offend not in word, the same is a perfect man, and able also to bridle the whole body. Behold, we put bits in the horses' mouths, that they may obey us; and we turn about their whole body. Behold also the ships, which though they be so great, and are driven of fierce winds, yet are they turned about with a very small helm, whithersoever the governor listeth. Even so the tongue is a little member, and boasteth great things. Behold, how great a matter a little fire kindleth! And the tongue is a fire, a world of iniquity: so is the tongue among our members, that it defileth the whole body, and setteth on fire the course of nature; and it is set on fire of hell' – James 3:2-6

Recognize the place of the tongue and use it to create peace and not war. Use it to create peace that 'passeth all understanding'. Don't use it to keep one party awake and the other one snoring all night. Build your home with kind words and take responsibility for all your words and actions. Don't be derogatory in your words concerning your wife. Be positive in your words. Speak to bring peace and unity. Be sensitive and responsive. Let words of your mouth bring hope and comfort. Your marriage will wax stronger and stronger all the way. Amen!

Keep Developing

Marriage is a DEVELOPMENT PLAN. Couples that don't realize this will waste their years in poverty. Big things start small and grow big. Marriage is a big thing. Coca-Cola didn't start big. It started small in a little kettle. Today, after adding one more ingredient called 'imagination' and had the liquid content bottled, there are over one billion consumers. Coca-Cola is the biggest consumer of sugar in the world today. When Asa Candler bought the formula from the originating Pharmacist, he added his imagination to bottle it. This was a development plan. Today, Coca-Cola is a global phenomenon.

Your marriage is a development plan just as you were. You started out as a tiny little spermatozoa, met an X female egg and you were fertilized. Born after nine months, you are a full grown today. You are married now (if you are). You were a development plan in the hands of your parents. Develop your marriage. Study about marriage, how to raise children, how to make your spouse happy and how to make the home work! Invest your time and resources to develop this great institution.

You started out as man and wife. Children will be (must have been) added. Your finances will take a new level of growth if you will navigate the vicissitudes of life victoriously. Work at it. Grow your finances to meet the impending challenges of life. Don't be static, grow and become successful in every aspect of life. Remember one thing, MARRIAGE IS A DEVELOPMENT PLAN. Start small but grow big!

Always Agree

73

The enemy will always want to add a prefix (DI) to the 'vision' of your marriage. You cannot afford 'di-vision' if you must see your love for each other last until you watch your children's marriages last forever. The devil will fight to prevent spouses from reaching agreement to sit down and talk. Soon division sets in as the children begin to take sides with parents. Beware of the devices and divisive tendencies of the devil.

If you must disagree, only disagree to agree. Agreement to sit down and talk is the antidote to the hideous overtures of the devil. So, sit down to talk and talk to agree. There is power in agreement. Agree to make progress. The Bible says two are better than one. If two of you are on the same page, victory is certain. Look at the agreement between Abraham and Sarah:

> *'And yet indeed she is my sister; she is the daughter of my father, but not the daughter of my mother; and she became my wife. And it came to pass, when God caused me to wander from my father's house, that I said unto her, This is thy kindness which thou shalt shew unto me; at every place whither we shall come, say of me, He is my brother'* – Gen. 20:12-13

They conquered Abimelech eventually. God endorsed their agreement and gave them victory. The place of agreement is the place of power. Marriage is a platform for agreement and power. God will always honour the agreement of couples and deliver them in the days of trouble, Abraham and Sarah, for example.

'Verily I say unto you, Whatsoever ye shall bind on earth shall be bound in heaven: and whatsoever ye shall loose on earth shall be loosed in heaven. Again I say unto you, That if two of you shall agree on earth as touching anything that they shall ask, it shall be done for them of my Father which is in heaven' – Matt. 18:18-19

Follow the Right Model and Be a Good Model Too

74

Which of these two grandfathers was a better model: David the father of Solomon or Abraham the father of Isaac? Between the two sons, who of them had a successful marriage and whose marriage can be said to be a good model? Who would you choose as the right model: a man who built God a house and immorally acquired 700 wives and 300 concubines or a man whose father had a great marriage and who picked a wife from where his father got his own wife?

David had a dysfunctional family. His marriage cannot be said to be a good model. His son too had a marriage that nobody till date has emulated. He had 1000 women. On the other hand, Abraham had a firm control over his family. God called him his friend because he ran a united and godly family. Isaac, his son too had a great marriage in spite of the delay in child birth. They stayed united and God blessed them with the fruit of the womb.

Do you want to revolutionize your marriage and make it great and positive? Follow the right model: Abraham and Isaac. Don't follow the wrong one. Marriage is not between one man and many women like that of David and Solomon. It is not also between one woman and many men like we see in our society today. An ideal marriage is between one man and one woman. Abraham and Isaac met this standard. And they stuck to their partners in spite of many years of trusting God for the fruit of the womb. Do two things to have a great marriage: Choose the right model and be a good model yourself!

Train Your Children to Train Their Own Children

75

You have not succeeded if your successor has not succeeded. Your duty as parents should transcend your immediate family. Teach your children good and godly values but train them too. Train them by practical demonstration of what you are teaching them. Training is a step further teaching. Teaching instructs, training demonstrates. Children will learn better by practical demonstration.

> 'And the things that thou hast heard of me among many witnesses, the same commit thou to faithful men, who shall be able to teach others also' – 2 Tim. 2:2

Apostle Paul applied this method of committing the truth to faithful men who committed it to other faithful men also. Train your children and watch them train their children. Remember, example is better than precepts. Train them to do those things that will make God proud of you and them. Train them to love their wives and respect their husbands. Train them to be kindhearted and gentle. Train them to love God with all their heart. Train them to study the Bible, fast and pray. Train them to be the ideal children, spouses and parents that you are!

Let God Be Your Ultimate Focus

'Jesus answered and said unto him, Verily, verily, I say unto thee, Except a man be born again, he cannot see the kingdom of God Jesus answered and said unto him, Verily, verily, I say unto thee, Except a man be born again, he cannot see the kingdom of God. Nicodemus saith unto him, How can a man be born when he is old? can he enter the second time into his mother's womb, and be born? Jesus answered, Verily, verily, I say unto thee, Except a man be born of water and of the Spirit, he cannot enter into the kingdom of God. That which is born of the flesh is flesh; and that which is born of the Spirit is spirit. Marvel not that I said unto thee, Ye must be born again. The wind bloweth where it listeth, and thou hearest the sound thereof, but canst not tell whence it cometh, and whither it goeth: so is every one that is born of the Spirit.' – John 3:3-8

Nicodemus was a highly placed personality in the Jewish society. He was one of the religious gladiators. He came to Jesus by night but Jesus did not hesitate to hit the nail at the head. He told him point blank: YOU MUST BE BORN AGAIN. He made him to know that being Born Again is the first prerequisite of seeing the Kingdom of God. The Kingdom of God should be your ultimate goal. So, in your marriage, have the bigger picture in your mind. Your marriage is capable of pushing you into or pulling you out of the Kingdom of God. Why did Jesus emphasize the matter of being BORN AGAIN to Nicodemus? The Kingdom of God! This is our ultimate goal and abode. Remember: there shall be another marriage hereafter; the marriage of the Lamb and His bride, the Church!

Your Marriage Must Be Born Again

77

Do not hesitate to get your marriage born again. To be born again is to be born anew; to align with God; to be under the modus operandi of the word of God. Just as you are born again, see to it that your marriage is born again. See to it that your marriage is born of the water and Spirit. What does water stand and Spirit stand for?

> 'That he might sanctify and cleanse it with the washing of water by the word' – Eph. 5:26

> 'It is the spirit that quickeneth; the flesh profiteth nothing: the words that I speak unto you, they are spirit, and they are life' – John 6:63

The Water and Spirit stand for the WORD of God. Let your marriage be born again; born of the WORD of God. Let your marriage follow the dictates of the WORD of God! There are many things in this world today that negate the WORD of God. Examples are same sex marriage, divorce and remarriage, homosexuality, lesbianism, transgender, gay, pornography. All these negate the WORD of God. Move your marriage far away from them and make it BORN AGAIN by Water and Spirit which is the WORD of God! This is how your marriage can be revolutionized.

Never Ever Forget Genesis 222

78

'And the rib, which the LORD God had taken from man, made he a woman, and brought her unto the man' – Gen. 2:22

According to Scriptures, God took a rib from Adam's side, fashioned a woman out of it and brought her to him. Never ever forget this process in Genesis chapter 2 verse 22. There are two great lessons to learn here: one for the men and the other for the women. To the men: Never ever forget that it is God who identified the incompleteness of Adam and brought Eve to him. So, God is involved in your marriage with your spouse, no matter what. To the women, never ever forget that it was God who brought Eve to Adam. She didn't flaunt herself so cheaply around Adam like girls do today. She didn't throw herself cheaply on the arms of Adam. It was God who brought her to Adam. While the man should not forget that God identified his deficiency and brought a woman to fill it, the woman should not throw herself immorally at men's feet. Know your worth!

Respect God's Gift

Eve was God's gift to Adam. The Bible says God brought her to the man. What do you do with gifts? You cherish them of course. Each time you see such gift, you remember the giver. The woman is God's gift to the man. Cherish her. Treat your wife with respect and value bearing in mind that God brought her to you.

When the gift leaves the hand of the owner to the hand of the receiver, it is the receiver who now takes responsibility as the custodian of the gift. God has given you your wife as a gift. Take full responsibility and nourish her. Maintain the worth and value God place on her. She is created after the image and likeness of God too. She has the Spirit of God. She is an heir of salvation through Christ Jesus. She is a perpetuator of mankind. Take proper care of God's gift in your hand!

Remember You Will Account For Your Allocation

80

In the beginning, the Lord did the selection and ignited a supernatural connection. Your wife is God's daughter allocated to you in trust, to love and to hold until the day of reckoning. Some people abuse their allocation and stretch out their neck elsewhere to greedily look for another. Keep your allocation carefully because you will give account of how you used or abused it.

Allocations don't grow and yield dividends if you are on a squandering spree. Sooner or later, it will deplete to an abysmal level. Your wife is your allocation, don't squander her. Don't deplete or erode her value. Water your lawn and keep it green so that you will not desire another man's green lawn. You must do all you can to improve her. Allocations are expected to yield dividends. There are a lot of benefits bottled up in your wife. Love and hold her; cherish and water her; value and excavate her until your house is full of the benefits and blessings of God. May you not squander but invest her to be profitable!

Take Your Marriage Seriously

81

Eve was brought to Adam in the Garden of Eden. Every man meets his wife at one point or the other. It may have been through meeting in a bus, taxi, park, library, dance floor, shopping mall, home church or gas station. It is all by God's grand design. Just as God brought Eve to Adam, God makes the path of a man and his wife cross. Therefore, take your marriage seriously. It doesn't matter that you married as an unbeliever or you met your wife in a night club or cinema. Now that you are a born again Christian, go ahead and take your marriage to that girl seriously.

If any man is in Christ, he is a new creature; old things are passed away and things become new (2 Cor. 5:1`7). This does not include your spouse. You don't throw out your spouse when you throw out old ways of life. Take your spouse to the zone of new things; to the arena of all things have become new. So, take your marriage seriously.

Affirm Your Spouse

82

'And Adam said, This is now bone of my bones, and flesh of my flesh: she shall be called Woman, because she was taken out of Man' – Gen. 2:23

When God brought Eve to him, Adam said, this is now bone of my bones, and flesh of my flesh: she shall be called Woman, because she was taken out of Man. This was an affirmation. He affirmed her and gave her a name that has remained with her till date. He had this understanding and verbalized it to her hearing. God gave us an example of this sort of affirmation too:

'And lo a voice from heaven, saying, This is my beloved Son, in whom I am well pleased' – Matt. 3:17

'While he yet spake, behold, a bright cloud overshadowed them: and behold a voice out of the cloud, which said, This is my beloved Son, in whom I am well pleased; hear ye him' – Matt. 17:5

God made a strong affirmation about Jesus twice: the first time at River Jordan during baptism and the second time at the mountain of transfiguration. Remember John the Baptist also affirmed Jesus. His affirmation drew attention to Jesus immediately. Some people followed Jesus upon this affirmation.

'The next day John seeth Jesus coming unto him, and saith, Behold the Lamb of God, which taketh away the sin of the world' – John 1:29

'And looking upon Jesus as he walked, he saith, Behold the Lamb of God! And the two disciples heard him speak, and they followed Jesus' – John 1:36-37

Affirm her in your own words to her hearing like Adam did. Plant and imprint this understanding in your finite mind. Let her hear your affirmation and endorsement. Yes, affirm to her that you love her so dearly. Affirm your confidence and trust in her. Affirm she is half of you and you are half of her. Affirm to her that you are not complete without her. I think women enjoy this kind of affirmation. Give it to her over and over again. Moreover, affirm to her in the bedroom that you are a man!

Traditional Wedding is Necessary

83

Some people do not see the rationale behind traditional wedding. Wedding, whether traditional or white gives one definite assurance: that the man is not a boy but man enough to leave his father and mother. It assures the parents of the woman that he has left his own parents to cleave to their daughter (Genesis 2:24), a covenant in which he will become parent to their daughter.

I have said before that every man should behave like a father to his wife. The parents of the woman gave her out you in confidence and trust that you would play their role as parents henceforth. Husbands, see to this truth and don't betray the trust of your wife's parents. You are her new parent. Care for her like her father and mother. Prove that you are man enough to leave your father and mother to cleave to her. Prove to her that you can fill the gap her father left. This is one sure way to make your marriage great and positive.

Your Wife Also Received Something From God

'And out of the ground the LORD God formed every beast of the field, and every fowl of the air; and brought them unto Adam to see what he would call them: and whatsoever Adam called every living creature, that was the name thereof. And Adam gave names to all cattle, and to the fowl of the air, and to every beast of the field; but for Adam there was not found an help meet for him. And the LORD God caused a deep sleep to fall upon Adam and he slept: and he took one of his ribs, and closed up the flesh instead thereof; And the rib, which the LORD God had taken from man, made he a woman, and brought her unto the man' – Gen. 2:19-22

Cast back your mind to the story of creation. The Bible says God put Adam to sleep, cut his side, took out a rib and made her out of it after closing back the side which He cut. Furthermore, God gave Adam the power of an Attorney. Adam was the first Zoologist. He had the powers to call each animal whatever name he deemed fit and God endorsed it. He wielded enormous power and control in the Garden but God did not leave the woman empty handed. He gave her something: 'the power of influence'. It is like making the man the head and the woman the neck. You know how closely related the head is with the neck. You also know that the neck is capable of changing the direction of the head. So, men, be careful, women have influence. They can influence your powers either negatively or positively. Women, be careful too. Don't abuse your power of influence!

Remember She is a Suitable Help

85

'And the LORD God said, It is not good that the man should be alone; I will make him an help meet for him. And out of the ground the LORD God formed every beast of the field, and every fowl of the air; and brought them unto Adam to see what he would call them: and whatsoever Adam called every living creature, that was the name thereof. And Adam gave names to all cattle, and to the fowl of the air, and to every beast of the field; but for Adam there was not found an help meet for him' – Gen. 2:18-20

Each time you look at your wife, see her as she is: a help suitable, fit and appropriate for you. Men who have this divine understanding get the best out of their marriage. When they need someone to encourage them, they turn to her. When they need a confidant, they look at the other side of the bed. When they are famished, they knock at the kitchen door where she is lord. When they need true companion, they resort to her. When they need emotional satisfaction, they enter the bedroom instead of club houses. When they need to procreate according to divine command, they turn to her. She is always there to provide one kind of help another! Moreover, they understand according to scriptures that she is not only a suitable help but a sure source of favor from the Lord!

'Whoso findeth a wife findeth a good thing, and obtaineth favour of the LORD' – Proverbs 18:22

Explore the Good Thing in Your Home

86

'*Whoso findeth a wife findeth a good thing, and obtaineth favour of the LORD*' – Proverbs 18:22

God brought you a good thing expecting you to explore it to have His favor. It takes hard work, love and patience to achieve this. It is your prerogative to explore the good thing God gave to you. The acronym GOOD THING means:

G - Gracious
O - Outstanding
O - Object of love
D – Desirable
T – Trustworthy
H – Happiness
I – Important
N- Noble
G – Gold

Instead of seeing your wife as a trouble maker or the witch that is hindering you from making progress, see her as God sees her. God sees her as a GOOD THING. He says the day you find a wife is the day you find a good thing. The consequence of this is favor of the Lord. If you desire a great marriage, look at her from God's perspective. She is gracious, outstanding and an object of love. She is desirable, trustworthy and given to you to bring happiness if you do love and care for her. She is important to you, noble to the family and gold to be excavated. If you see her as a good thing, you will have the most of her: the favor of the Lord.

Continue the Relationship

87

One of the greatest undoing of couples is lack of continuity. Some people start well but fail to continue in the good way. In other words, they start well but end badly. Don't do what people like this do. They opt or back out of the good pattern and pick up strange habits or walk out of the relationship. You may be two steps away from the GOLD you are excavating. In the book, THINK AND GROW RICH by Napoleon Hill, Uncle Darby quit just when he was two feet away from gold after much investment in money, time and energy. The man that bought the equipment hit the gold zone after digging only two feet more. He had consulted an expert who told him he was only two feet away from gold.

We have an expert in God who is the originator of marriage. Don't quit! Dig a little more and you will find the gold that she is. Continue in your investment. Love more, be more patient and tolerant. Forgive again, give more money, time and attention. You are a few steps away from the reward zone!

Pray With and For Her

88

'And Isaac was forty years old when he took Rebekah to wife, the daughter of Bethuel the Syrian of Padan-aram, the sister to Laban the Syrian. And Isaac intreated the LORD for his wife, because she was barren: and the LORD was entreated of him, and Rebekah his wife conceived' – Gen. 25:20-21

Your spouse is your compulsory prayer partner. Pray together always to build a great marriage and family. There is a saying that the family that prays together stays together. Remember the Bible says if two shall agree on a matter, God will hear and answer them. You and your wife are the two that must agree in prayers. So, agree and pray with your wife.

There was several years of delay in child bearing when Isaac married Rebecca. One day, Isaac did the needful. The Bible says he entreated, implored or besought God on her behalf. He had been praying with her but this day, he made it a personal duty. He stepped up his prayer by pleading passionately for God to open her womb and God answered his prayers. Women do not like delay in anything, especially child bearing. Pray for her. Ask God to take away any kind of delay on her way. You both deserve to be happy. Make this happen on your knees!

Be Courteous, Firm and Friendly

89

Some people lack respect and decorum when they communicate. Their gesture and words depict impoliteness and disrespect. Disrespecting your spouse is disrespecting yourself. So, speak with a tinge of politeness. Don't be coarse and unnecessarily authoritative. Be respectful in making your point. Be firm and friendly and friendly but firm.

Be firm and friendly: let your firmness not be coarse or abrasive but friendly. In other words, let your firmness be friendly; lovingly exhibited; pleasantly expressed. Let your firmness not be seen to be antagonistic. Put your feet on the ground but lovingly and pleasantly. Let your NO be friendly. Let your WAIT be pleasant.

Be friendly but firm: let your friendliness have a tinge of firmness. In your friendliness, be assertive. On the hand, let your friendliness be real and not pretentious. On the other hand, let it not be misconstrued for weakness. Meekness is not weakness. Let the two attributes: friendliness and firmness be dominant. You will build a better relationship if they are.

Help Her to Be Submissive

The Bible is crystal clear about love and submission. The man is charged to love his wife as Christ loved the Church. The woman is also charged to respect and submit to her husband in all things. If she has issues with submission, kindly help her by loving her until she learns to submit. Tea bags are fantastic but until you bring it to boil in a kettle of water, it will not extract out the much needed ingredients and color. Sometimes, you may have to bring her top boil by hot love. Let your love for her be seething hot and then her submission will be extracted like a tea bag and there will be abundant of her respect and submission in your ego kitty. Women find it easy to submit but in case she has issues with submission, do exactly what I have just told you and you will reap a bumper harvest. She will submit to you until you in turn submit to her. Love is magical. It can turn an enemy into a friend, a nagging woman into a noble woman and a bitter spouse into a sweet one.

Let Peace Prevail

'And the earth was without form, and void; and darkness was upon the face of the deep. And the Spirit of God moved upon the face of the waters' – Gen. 1:2

The Bible says the earth was chaotic. It was without. The Message Bible calls it a soup of nothingness; a bottomless emptiness; an inky blackness. But God did something about this chaotic situation. The Bible says the Spirit of God moved, brooded or hovered upon the waters and solution was proffered. There was peace at the end of the tunnel and everything God did was referred to as good.

There is something you can do in a chaotic situation in your home. Think of brooding and hovering too like your Father in heaven. Strain yourself to let peace prevail. Go the extra mile to bring peace. Go beyond limits to ensure that peace reigns in the family. Learn from Abraham who curried peace at all cost with Lot and his herdsmen. There is blessedness in making peace. The Bible says blessed are the peacemakers for they shall see God. Let there be a restraining order on discord in the family by both parties. There shall be Shalom!

Aim at Your Spouse Loving You Like a Dog

92

'And be ye kind one to another, tenderhearted, forgiving one another, even as God for Christ's sake hath forgiven you' – Eph. 4:32

'Forbearing one another, and forgiving one another, if any man have a quarrel against any: even as Christ forgave you, so also do ye' – Col. 3:13

Forgiveness is a divine virtue. It is strength to forgive. Marriage is a union between two forgiven people charged with the mandate to forgive and forbear. The dog has this virtue and a lot of it. Love forgives, forbears and forgets. Dogs are forgiving. Even when you hurt them, they know their responsibility towards you as you come under attack or when there is an intruder. Dogs will not nurse a grudge to leave you in danger. They will still alert and protect you.

One of my friends, John, in Nigeria, Africa will always forgive his wife, Sarah by driving out and buying a gift for her. That gift is his symbol of forgiveness even without waiting for 'I am sorry' from her lips. He will go the extra mile to discharge his responsibility in spite of a misunderstanding. It is fine to forgive but buying a gift when offended is going the extra mile I am talking about. Try this out, when your spouse offends you, love like a dog, go out there and come back home with a gift. The offender will be amazed at your action. This is what God does for us. He still blesses us in spite of our misdemeanours.

Be Protective Like a Dog

93

Dogs will always strive to move forward and ahead of you to sense and avert danger. Sometimes, they leash behind to cover you from danger. This creature is an epitome of unconditional, sacrificial and absolute love. A dog is prepared to shed its blood for its owner or members of the household.

A dog can save the owner from an accident. Nobody loves and cares for children like dogs. Dogs turn the darkness of the blind into light by taking the lead. They never ever forsake the person they are leading, even unto death. They are a help to the helpless autistic child in times of need. Dogs are also ever present and ready to render unselective services to humans they are familiar with.

Learn to be protective like a dog. Protect, preserve and project your spouse. Be her wall of defence. Love and security are two prime desires of a woman. Just like God gives His angels charge over us so we do not dash our foot against a stone, so guard your wife jealously from danger and trouble. Jesus will always protect His bride, the church. Always protect your own bride too. This is one way you can revolutionize your marriage and make it positive!

Always Leave Indelible Marks

94

Radicalizing your marriage is a deliberate effort. One of the things you can do to make your marriage radicalized and positive is to always strive to leave a strong positive impression in the mind of your spouse. Leave indelible marks like a dog. You see, dogs leave indelible marks that enhance remembrance and serve as a reference point. When walking the dog, it insists in passing urine along the road. This way, he will smell your way back when you miss the road. Pass the urine of love, good works, generosity, patience, kindness, tolerance, forgiveness, compromise, gentleness, etc. You will always be remembered for these virtues. Even when your spouse is mad at you, she will remember your good aspects! He will remember your impact in his life!

Like a Dog, Retain the Aroma of Your Spouse

95

Dogs! They retain the smell of your body. They remember the sound of your car. They know the horn of your car. They decipher them from afar as you return and wait to give you a rousing welcome at the door! You can do better than the dog. Retain the details about your spouse. Know her choice of clothing, shoes and bags. Know the size of her underclothes, the type of chocolate she relishes, the flowers, the pastries and all those things ladies adore. Know his choice of colour, his shoe size, the caps, T-shirts, snickers and all those things he appreciates. Each time you get the right gifts, you cement your relationship the more. Buying gifts for your spouse is not enough, they must be what are appreciated!

Like A Dog, Wait on Your Spouse

96

As if retaining the smell of the owner is not enough or the grand welcome is not sufficient, the dog will sit down near the couch close to the owner and await any other orders. We have been principally charged to wait on the Lord in order to renew our strength like the eagle. Waiting upon the Lord is not only fasting and prayer. It also means to wait like a waiter in the restaurant to take orders from the Lord. Like the dog besides the owner, stay beside your owner like a waiter. Your husband owns you. Your wife owns you. Wait on each other like a waiter. Take orders and strive to outdo each other in service. This is one certain way to revolutionize, radicalize, reanimate and rekindle your marriage!

Reserve a Special Welcome

97

Dogs! They welcome you home 'lively' with constant jumping and wagging of the tail hilariously. They are happy and excited that you are back home! Reserve a special welcome for your spouse always. You can device your style of welcome. Some people plant a kiss on the forehead, cheeks or lips to say welcome. Others give a hug, a pat at the back or a seductive smile. The choice is exclusively yours! Tired, wearied and worn out, your spouse will feel excited on the way home when he remembers a special welcome awaits him at home by his lovely wife. In spite of the whirl of activities in the work place, she will feel elated on her way home when she remembers a special welcome awaits her by her lovely husband. Always make reservations that bring refreshments!

Keep Excitement High

98

With dogs, there are no dull moments. They are always jumping around, kissing and licking the owner's feet. This is a positive approach. You too, maintain this poise. Jump around your spouse excitedly. Kiss and fondle with each other always. Life is a rhythm of mood. There are happy moments and there are sad ones. You can choose to be happy always. Keep excitement high! Don't let people or circumstances dictate your mood. Take charge of your emotions. You have the prerogative of power over your life. Keep excitement high. Say NO to sad moments. Be Glad, don't be sad. Be merry, don't be moody.

Don't be cynical or sarcastic. Don't be overrun by worries. Be anxious for nothing. Guard your marriage jealously from sad and dull moments. You can maintain inner poise even in unpleasant circumstances. It is a deliberate effort you must make. The Bible says a merry heart doeth good like a medicine: but a broken spirit drieth the bones (Prov. 17:22). The Message Bible says: 'a cheerful disposition is good for your health; gloom and doom leave your bone tired'. So, be merry always. Have a cheerful disposition. Keep excitement high!

Generously Express Your Love

Again like a dog, express your love for your spouse generously. Dogs are very generous in expression of love. They do not hide it when their owner is around. Be magnanimous in the expression of your love. There are many ways you can express your love. Please, do so generously. You can express your love verbally by telling him or her, 'I love you'. Say it and mean it by practicing it. You can express your love by doing laundry for your wife. You can express your love by cooking for her before she returns from work if you get home before her. You can express your love by doing what your spouse should normally do. Be generous in this love expression. Moreover, be generous in the bedroom! Let her feel like a woman. Let him feel like a man. As long as your health or strength permits!

Pay the Price for Continuity

Marriage commitment is a two way thing. The man and woman must be committed to ensure continuity. There is something special about the dog. They are always prepared to pay the price of continuity in relationship. First, they keep their part of the bargain by playing their roles dutifully. Second, they do not forsake the owner and walk away. You too, strive to pay the price for continuity. Do not push your partner to the wall to think of discontinuing the relationship. And when you are pushed to the wall, do not think of discontinuing. Two things here: don't push the other and when you are pushed, don't discontinue. Let continuity be your dictum.

Be Whores to Each Other

101

When it comes to intimacy, be whores to each other. There is nothing wrong with prostituting with each other. Be seductive to yourselves as much as you can. Kindle the fire of passionate sex. Give it to each other without holding back. The Bible talks of submitting to each other (Eph. 5:21) and orders the wife to submit to her husband (Eph. 5:22). The wife is also required to submit to her husband in *'all things'* (Eph. 5:24).

Submit yourself to your husband in the bedroom. Let him be the master and driver. Remember the Bible says 'in all things'. This includes bedroom activities. Let him have his fill. Satisfy him, breast feed him like his mother use to do when he was a baby and let him feel overwhelmed with your love. Husband, don't rejoice too quickly because I said you are the master and driver in the bedroom. Remember Ephesians 5:21 talks of mutual submission. You are required to submit one to another. So, submit to her also as the queen of the bedroom. Let her be the mistress and driver. She can be in charge of proceedings in the bedroom. She can choose to be atop, underneath or beside. The choice is hers. Make love to satisfaction whenever you want it. In a nutshell, be whores to each other.

Printed in the United States
by Baker & Taylor Publisher Services